WHAT THEY TEACH YOU AT THE WHARTON BUSINESS SCHOOL

HOW TO BE AN ENTREPRENEUR, START A SUCCESSFUL BUSINESS, SELL MORE THAN THE COMPETITION, MAKE MORE MONEY, HAVE MORE FUN, BE A BETTER PERSON, AND LIVE A HAPPIER LIFE

CLINT ARTHUR

John, follow your Heart!

Published by Ivy League Entrepreneur Books
New York • Las Vegas • Los Angeles

For Reprint or Special Sales CONTACT
Clint Arthur • Ivy League Entrepreneur Books
5348 Vegas Drive • Las Vegas • NV • 89108
TEL (702)987-0113 • FAX (702)938-8618
www.FreeNewPower.com

This book is dedicated to the entrepreneurial spirit
and the freedom which it creates.

CONTENTS

ACKNOWLEDGMENTS

I am most grateful to my many friends and teachers who have guided me along my path and helped me to become the man I am today:

Myles Bass, Frank McCourt, Matt Litwin, Dr. Robert Sharon, Dr. Stuart Glassman, Arthur Linder, Doug Palczewski, Mike Ognibene, John Yuder, Tommy Leonardi, Nick Bazarini, Brian Ross, Dr. Sam Fager, John Favreau, Hillary Frankel, Stu Frankel, Phil Timon, Todd Simon, Jono Steinberg, David Rothschild, Tommy Frayne, Bob Massick, Paul Fennouillet, Bill Harrington, Kevin Goldberg, Mike Weiss, Erik Rothenberg, Lynelle Kerstine, Robert Gross, Jeff Herman, Arnold Dolin, Charles Sherman, Dan Engel, Brock Harris, David Andersen, Dylan Stewart, Mark Brems, Martin Hannon, Danny Lembo, Barry Gershenson, Eduardo Santana, Ed Ellman, Gregory Gourreau, Mimmo Bruno, Scott Imsland, Jean-Georges Vongerichten, Dan Del Vecchio, Vincent Pouessel, David Werly, Edmond Wong, Vittorio Giordano, Jason Harrison, Ana Marie Mormando, Martin Heierling, Eric Damidot, Julian Serrano, Ryland Worrell, Robert Moore, Sean Griffin, John Gresty, Tom Passantino, Olivier Dubreuil, Jacques Van Staden, Rosemary Low, Andre Rochat, Jean-Louis Palladin, George Noory, Prof. E. Digby Baltzell, Susan and everyone at Annie Jennings PR, Brent Roske, Takashi Murakami, James Malinchak, Justin Sterling, Denny Gregg, Mark Victor Hansen, Paul Allen, Don Miguel Ruiz, Brendon Burchard, Donald Trump, Tony Robbins, Paul Roth, Mom & Dad, my amazing wife Alison, and my daughter, for whom I wrote this book.

INTRODUCTION

It's been 24 years since I graduated from the Wharton Business School.

Back in 1987 you could get a 4-year Wharton education for the bargain basement price of about $100,000. Today that same education would cost you somewhere in the realm of $250,000 -- one quarter of a million dollars.

Over these 2+ decades, I've thought to myself many times, What were the most important things that I got from my hundred grand investment, for my four years of time, for the sweat, the toil, the heartache?

I wrote down several lists: Top 10 things I Learned at the Wharton Business School... Most Important Things I Learned at Wharton... and I always intended to write a book about it, but I never sat down and wrote it because it never felt like the right time.

I went on a leadership retreat recently, and the theme of this event was "Our days are numbered." With the perspective of that event, I got my perspective on this book.

I realized that I want to immortalize the lessons I learned and the wisdom I've gained so that one day in the future, after I'm dead and gone, when my little 13 year-old daughter is all grown up, she'll be able to turn to this volume for wisdom, for guidance, and for the most help I can possibly give her.

So congratulations to you! You have discovered something that is worth far in excess of $250,000 because 1) you won't have to pay all that money for it; 2) you don't have to take your time to actually sit through the 4 years of classes; and 3) it's condensed into this really tight format that you can take with you in your iPhone or laptop and read at your leisure, anywhere you want.

So let's get started! Here's the best stuff from a top student at the best business school in the world...

Enjoy!

Sincerely,

Clint Arthur

1

INSPIRE YOURSELF

My Wharton education began when I was 14 years old. I was reading a novel. It was a story about a phenomenally successful businessman who had attended and graduated from something called the Wharton Business School in Philadelphia. It was rated the top business school in the world, even better than Harvard Business School.

Right then and there, when I was 14 years old, I made up my mind: I'm going to go to the Wharton Business School.

From that point in my life, everything was guided by going to Wharton.

I knew that you needed to have above 1300 on your SAT scores, so I went to Kaplan's test preparation course for the PSAT's and for the SAT's – my priorities in life were totally focused on getting above 1300 on the SAT's, which was the median SAT score for accepted applicants to Wharton.

Attending Kaplan's meant that I had to be in classes at 930am on Saturday mornings for most of 10th and 11th grade.

Despite the fact that I positively hate waking up early, and I had to travel 45 minutes to get there by subway, I never missed a single class at Kaplan's.

That's the kind of goals you need to set for yourself: the kind that can get you out of bed in the morning because they are so exciting and inspiring to you.

I also knew that successful applicants did a lot of extra-curricular activities, so I did varsity sports, I was the star of school plays, I became the business manager of our high school newspaper and the treasurer of the student union. Because I knew that they wanted those things.

I hated my home when I was growing up. The TV was always blaring, my parents were always fighting, and it was tough to concentrate. So at night when I wanted to study or concentrate intensely on my homework, I would go down the street and sneak in to the NYU dental school library. Once inside, I would get down into the depths of the stacks and do my homework.

Whenever I needed some extra motivation, I would look at the college guidebooks and open up the listing for the University of Pennsylvania's Wharton School. I would look at what the scores were, over and over and over -- and when I was done looking at the scores I would buckle down and do my work because I knew that I needed to be a top student since Wharton only took the very best.

I must've looked at those statistics a hundred times over sophomore, junior, and senior years in high school. Even though I knew the scores by heart, I would open the book and look at the numbers in black and white, time after time –

because I was obsessed with getting into Wharton.

I was like a religious zealot. Getting into Wharton was like my religion. It was my constant guiding light.

When it came time to apply to college, of course I applied early decision to Wharton. The rule was you could only apply to one school early decision, and if you were accepted, you had to go. I never even once considered wavering or not applying early decision. I was totally committed and focused on the goal.

Came December, I got a big fat envelope from the University of Pennsylvania, and inside that envelope was an acceptance letter and congratulations from the Dean of Admissions, welcoming me to the Class of 1987.

I filled out 1 application for college, and it was over. It was a done deal, I was going to Wharton – all because I set an inspirational goal for myself and pursued that goal with passion.

2

THE POWER OF LOVE

The 2nd secret of success I learned at the Wharton Business School was the importance of people loving you.

People Loving You is the most important thing in the world; and with regard to the Wharton School, it's how I got in!

I remember the day that I went to my alumni interview; it was a fall afternoon during my Senior year of high school, I put on my best preppy clothing so that I looked like I was an Ivy League kind of guy, and I walked over to the alumni interviewer's apartment across town, over on 5th Avenue and 22nd street.

The doorman let me in, then I went up to an apartment on the 20th floor and rang the bell. The door opened and the interviewer was very happy and excited when he said "Hi! I'm Greg." He shook my hand, and said, "Come in and have a seat."

I sat down, and he said "You know, I really have to admit something to you."

I said "Really, what's that Greg?"

"Well, I'm Broadway producer, and what I like to do in my spare time is to keep up with the local High School productions, especially the musicals. I saw you when you were Conrad Birdie in Bye Bye Birdie at Stuyvesant High School and you were fantastic!"

Right there I knew I was a shoe-in. <u>The guy loved me</u> because of my performance in that play, which dovetails right into the whole concept I explained earlier about being a well-rounded person and having all kinds of extra-curricular activities. Once again my education at Wharton was being drummed into me before I ever even got to Wharton.

*****

Now let me give you an example of how important it is for people to love you that I learned when I was a student at the Wharton School.

When I started pledging my fraternity, Psi Upsilon (aka The Castle aka The Coolest Fraternity In The Entire History of College Fraternities,) a new President had been elected by the brotherhood just prior to Winter Break, and his name was Keith Olsen.

Keith Olsen was everything that any man could ever want the President of his fraternity to be. A great-looking guy with a perfect smile, good skin, a firm handshake, steady gaze, great understated preppy clothes, a guy who would drink a beer or a gin and tonic with you, shoot a game of pool with you, he could pick up chicks, go gambling in Atlantic City, he was glad to sing fraternity songs out on the front steps and boogie down at our legendary Studio-54-esque house parties. He was also in the US Navy R.O.T.C. program and ended up flying fighter jets in the first Gulf War. That kind of guy. The kind of guy you wanted to be. The kind of guy you wanted to be your friend. A guy you couldn't help but love like a brother – because you admired him so much.

Then there was our rival fraternity, Saint A's, right up the street on Locust Walk, a very dark, mysterious chapter house exclusively full of true WASPy blue-bloods and aristocrats, as opposed to our house which was right out in the open, smack in the center of campus, and in reality a melting pot of races, religions, and economic strata. My friend Enrique Gallo (whose uncle was Samosa, the former dictator of Nicaragua,) was an A's brother, and though I really liked Enrique, and I was intrigued by All Things WASPy, I never felt any true interest in or connection to Saint A's – I think because the place lacked soul.

OK, so now you've got all the background, so here's the story: towards the end of our pledging period, I came up with the idea that we (the pledge class) were going to steal the Saint A's flag. It flew from a pole off a balcony on the 2nd floor of their house, and I figured we could cut it down with a long set of tree pruning shears. All the guys loved it, and the plan was set in motion for what would become one of the most memorable events of my entire college experience.

At about 2 in the morning, all 14 members of my pledge-class rendezvoused at The Castle, then made our way over to Saint A's with the pruning shears.

My brothers acted as lookouts as I climbed the tree which would allow me to reach the flag. It turned out to be a lot higher up in the air than it looked from the ground! Everything went perfectly, except for the fact that the shears were not strong enough to cut the rope bearing the Saint A's standard. I tried and I tried, but I just couldn't get enough leverage on the blades to cut it.

As I was up in the tree a Campus Security guard came along and asked what was going on – one of my brothers explained it was a fraternity prank, and the guard walked away with a shrug.

I came back down and surveyed the building to come up with another plan.

"Okay, here's what's going to happen," I said to the men as they stood around in the brisk night air. "You guys are going to boost me up onto the fire escape, then I'll go up to the top, climb up that downspout onto the roof, lower myself down onto the balcony with a rope and cut down their flag. Now all we need is a rope."

I spotted a hose on the side of the building, and the next thing I know I'm scrambling up the fire escape, then up the copper downspout, then across the roof, and then I'm tiptoeing over to the edge of the roof to survey the scene.

As I peeked my head over the parapet wall, I heard one of my pledge brothers exclaim in a loud whisper, "He's on the roof!"

My heart was racing, and I could hear the Saint A's flag snapping in wind on the balcony 15 feet below me. It was a long way down to the ground from the top of this 3-story building! Am I out of my mind? I wondered as I tied my hose around the triangular peak of the façade and dropped it over the side. I must be crazy! I thought to myself as I lowered myself Pink Panther-style down onto the balcony of some A's brother's room.

From there it was a simple matter of untying the flag and letting it drop into the eager hands of my brothers. I'm not really sure how I got out of there, but I did, and pretty soon we all re-convened in The Castle to figure out what would come next.

We had done it! We had stolen Saint A's flag! Now what?

We decided to wake up our Pledge Master and Keith Olsen and present them with the bootie.

Now the Pledge Master is an obvious choice. His name was Stricker Cole Sanford, III – Rick Sanford—and both his father and grandfather were brothers of The Castle before him. He was also a WASPy guy, also had good skin, a straight smile, decent clothes, and was ROTC, but interestingly, I didn't have that same love for Rick Sanford that I had for Keith. Yes, Rick was my Pledge Master, and I felt a special connection to him for that, but he was much more reserved and was missing a warmth and inner smile that Keith had which made him lovable. So we picked Rick because he was in charge of us, but we picked Keith because we looked up to him, we loved him, and <u>we wanted him to love each of us.</u>

It was a matter of stealing into their rooms, putting pillowcases over their heads, and secreting them down into the basement where we had Saint A's flag proudly hung on the barroom wall next to the pool table, brightly lit up with track spotlights. This was all very much in keeping with the regular kind of stuff that went on in our fraternity pledging process, so they went along with it and stood there until we told them to remove their pillow-cases.

Rick, being more reserved, didn't say anything, he just smiled. But Keith said "Alright! Way to go!"

Then we all went up to the roof and hoisted Saint A's flag on the pole which normally flew the Penn flag, and as the dawn started to break, we sang fraternity songs and basked in the glow of brotherly love.

That was a truly great moment, for myself, and for every man who was present. I know it must've been a great moment for Keith, because he was there, and he was with us, because we loved him. He got to be a part of that spot-weld moment only because we loved him.

*****

Now I'll give you an example of how being well loved has benefited me since I've graduated from Wharton. As President of the Five Star Butter Company, it's my job to go out and sell the butter, especially to the big accounts like Bellagio in Las Vegas.

Now, I don't know how I did it -- I think it was because I kept going back for years with my little butter samples talking to the chefs, getting them to know me, getting them to like me, having them see how much I believed in the product, having them see how much I was persistent and reliable in my word -- and over time I have developed a relationship with just about every chef at the Bellagio Resort in Las Vegas, where they love me.

I walk into the kitchens with no appointment, and instead of being tossed out on my ass like other vendors are for showing up un-expected, I get hugs, I get smiles, I get big happy exclamations like: "Clint! How are you?!"

This has enabled me to get to the position where just about every single piece of bread and butter that is served in the Bellagio is served with Five Star Butter. It's a lot of butter. It's very important to my business, to the Five Star Butter Company, and it's all because I'm loved by the chefs at Bellagio.

So I cannot stress it enough: the most important thing is for people to love you. And everything I know about the subject of being loved is in another book I wrote called "Free Your Love Now." That book goes into all the aspects of Love, and I honestly would advise everyone to check out that book and learn as much as possible about the subject of Love, but for the time being, I really want to address a couple of basic things about love that are simple and useful.

Number 1: If you want to be loved, study a dog or a cat. Check them out. They are masters at getting people to love them.

Follow their behavior, see what they do, try to pick up some of the aspects of lovable-ness exhibited by dogs and cats.

If you don't have one, get one. There's nothing you can do to get more in love in your life faster than to get yourself a dog or a cat.

Really a dog, more than a cat – but it depends on the cat.

We have a cat named Opal, who is the master of assuming the rapport. She just makes everyone who meets her fall in love with her. It's unbelievable! And mostly she does it by assuming the rapport. She just comes up and gets right in your face and she wants to be with you, and all of the sudden you want to be with her.

This issue of assuming the rapport -- that is a powerful tool which will be covered in depth as the subject of a later chapter -- basically it's the concept that if you act like a person is your friend, then they will be your friend. You just assume that they're your friend, and bam! They're your friend. You assume the rapport. I learned that in another class I took after graduating called "How to make anyone like you in 90 seconds or less." That was the whole secret of that class.

<u>Number 2:</u> I couldn't touch on the subject of love and being loved if I didn't really address this issue 100% <u>In order for other people to love you, you have to love yourself first.</u>

You have to be a person deserving of love from yourself.

<u>Before anyone else is going to love you.</u>

How do you do that?

How do you love yourself?

Well, if you really want to get into it, read the "Free Your Love Now" book. But a couple of simple starting ideas that I will suggest are these:

A: feeding yourself well. Providing your body with the best fuel you can get your hands on is a very subtle signal to yourself that you love yourself. And since you eat every day, it's a symbol that gets repeated and reinforced daily. It's also something that you see, touch, taste, feel, and sometimes hear, so it activates all your senses with a message that you love and value yourself.

B: being a good person, not an evil person. If you continuously do righteous and positive things for people and the world, you will admire and love yourself for it. The opposite is also true.

C: be an interesting person with genuine interests, passions, pursuits, hobbies, desires, goals. If all you do is watch television all day long, you are not going to inspire much love for yourself. But if you are a dynamic and interesting person, you will inspire yourself to respect and love yourself. You will also attract other people to you, which will reinforce your feelings of love.

And lastly, D: in order to really love yourself, you have to be a nice person. It's simple: be nice to yourself and to others. That's a loveable quality.

So be nice person, be interesting, take care of yourself, be interested in other people, and assume the rapport.

3

PEOPLE ARE EVERYTHING

Welcome to Chapter 3, and congratulations! You're going to get some incredible knowledge and information in this chapter. Information and knowledge that cost me 4 years of my life, and in excess of $100,000 in 1983 - '87 dollars (which is like a quarter of a million today) when I was a student at the Wharton Business School.

This chapter is packed with good stuff so lets get right to it.

In this chapter I'm going to talk about personnel.

People.

In one of my best classes at Wharton, in the Entrepreneurial Management Division, my professor's name was Myles Bass. The guy was just an entrepreneurial genius. A true dynamo. He used to say to us that he had 82 partners in business. That guy was just a moneymaking machine! I loved that guy!

One day he talked about this subject for a whole class. He wrote it up on the board: "personnel."

People.

People are everything.

They make things happen.

They come up with solutions.

The right people are people you can depend on.

They will make you money.

They will make money for you!

And more importantly than that, people are what make living fulfilling.

If there were no people, what would it all be worth? All you'd have would be yourself and a dog, or yourself and a cat, yourself and a goldfish...

It's the people in our lives that bring richness and fulfillment to life.

One of the most important things I want to make sure that my daughter understands from this project is that one of the most important things you get from your college education is the people that you're going to meet, become friends with, become associated with. Those people will change your life for the better -- and for the worse.

Let's start with my good buddy Dr. Stu.

Today, he's a teacher on the faculty of Dartmouth Medical School, but back in High School Dr. Stu was just Stu-Man-Stu, the boyfriend of a girl I knew from Madrigal Society in Junior High School. (Madrigal was a special chorus group that I belonged to which used to travel around New York City giving performances with musicians like Pete Fountain and his New Orleans Jazz Band.)

In high school, I wanted to go out for the gymnastics team, so I started going to the practices, and Dr. Stu was on the gymnastics team. He came over to me one day and he goes, "Hey you know my girlfriend, Jory from chorus, right?"

I'm like "Yeah."

And he says "Ok, well, she says you're a good guy, so we're gonna be friends."

I said, "Cool!" So we became friends. This was in the beginning of my freshman year.

One day at the beginning of my sophomore year of high school, Stu-Man-Stu comes up to me after school. As usual, people are hanging out in front of the building, just chilling out, seeing and being seen, and he says, "Hey man, you're a good singer, right?"

I said "Yeah."

He said, "How'd you like to be the star of the school play?"

I said "Sure." I'd been the star of a number of school plays before, in 5th, 6th, 7th, and 8th grades, so I was pretty casual about it.

He goes, "OK, come with me."

Stu brings me back inside the school, down into the auditorium. He was on the Stage Squad, (the people who are behind the scenes for the plays and productions of the school,) so he takes me up through the Stage Squad office and then out on to the stage where there's a whole gaggle of girls grouped around this man who I'd never met before.

His name was Mr. Litwin, and he was a Chemistry teacher at the school. This year, for the first and only time, Mr. Litwin was in charge of being the director of the school play (for some odd reason which never was explained.)

So Stu says, "Hey, Mr. Litwin, this is the guy I was telling you about."

Mr. Litwin looks at me and he goes, "Yeah... he looks like he could play the part. Can you sing?"

I said "Yeah."

He said, "Are you a good singer?"

I said, "Yeah."

He said, "Can you dance?"

I said, "Uh..."

He goes, "Can you just move your body in a decent way?"

I said, "I guess so, I'm on the gymnastics team."

He says, "How would you like to be Conrad Birdie in the school play? Conrad is like Elvis Presley, and all the girls are in love with him."

I smiled shyly and said, "I think I could do that."

Everybody laughed.

He said, "Ok well you have to have a formal audition of course, but I think you got the part."

Low and behold, I had my audition, I got the part, I went on to do a great job playing Conrad Birdie, and from that, as I told you in the previous chapter, I got into the Wharton Business School.

So, really, just because of a person I met in Junior High School, my whole life was completely changed. I went to the best business school in the world, I became an entrepreneurial management major, I studied with Myles Bass, and I learn the importance of Personnel.

*****

Here's another example from when I was a student at the University of Pennsylvania in the Wharton Business School:

You never know how you get to meet a person, sometimes you will set it up in your mind and say I want to meet this person, and then you go and meet this person and they'll have a big impact on your life. Other times, the meeting will be totally by random coincidence, and this example is exactly that.

When I was a student at Wharton I joined a fraternity that was the best fraternity, not just at the Wharton School or at the University of Pennsylvania, but of any fraternity in the whole world. This was the greatest fraternity. It was called The Castle, because it looked like a castle. That's right: we, the members of the brotherhood, lived in a castle. It was a blue-grey limestone fortress, and it was gorgeous, with turrets and wainscoting on the walls, and a huge stuffed elk head over the fireplace. Just an awesome fraternity!

One of my fraternity brothers in my Pledge Class was this guy named Evan. I really didn't like Evan. He was from California, and I thought he was too much into smoking pot and taking drugs, and not a serious student like I was, and he didn't seem like the kind of guy I wanted to be friends with.

But he was pledge brother of mine, we became brothers of the fraternity in the pledging process together, and then it came the end of the school year and it was time to figure out who would be living in which rooms in The Castle when we came back to school in the Fall.

In picking rooms, the way we did it in The Castle was to draw cards from a deck of regular playing cards, and the higher cards got the first pick, while the lower cards got last pick.

There were 4 single rooms in that building, and upper class brothers took those singles because they had seniority. Then the new brothers got to pick from what was left, so pretty much everybody in my pledge class had to have a roommate. The card I picked was the two of spades, the absolute lowest card in the deck.

People are pairing off -- because everybody had to pick a roommate -- and everybody picked their roommates before I did, so then it got to be that the only people who didn't pick roommates were me and this guy Evan.

So by process of pure default, I got teamed up to room with Evan.

Needless to say, Evan became one of my all time greatest and best friends. Not only did he bring a lot of joy and fun and great times to me and my life, but he also had a tremendous influence on what happened to me after college. Ultimately, it was because of my friendship with Evan that I moved to California, became a writer, and eventually, a real-estate developer.

You see, in New York you need to be a multi-millionaire in order to be a real-estate developer. Real-estate in New York is really expensive, and I come from very humble origins. My family was comfortable and middle-class, but by no means could you say we had a lot of money, because we didn't. And I never had a lot of money, until I became a real-estate developer.

The first time I went to California, I stayed with Evan's family at their mansion north of Sunset Boulevard in Beverly Hills. I arrived late at night, after his parents were already asleep. The next morning I went out to the pool, and there was his dad wearing a bathrobe, skimming paint off the top of the water of the pool with a pool-net. He had just had the edges of the pool painted, and there were some little paint blobs floating around.

He says, "Good Morning!"

I said, "Good morning."

"Welcome!"

I said, "Thank you, this is my first day in California."

He said, "You've never been to California before?"

I said, "Nope."

He said, "Ahhh! Welcome to Paradise."

I was 19 years old, and I immediately agreed with the man.

I did find California to be paradise, and although I moved around quite a bit in my 20's, I ended up coming out to California and pursuing a career as a writer, and ultimately getting into real-estate around the beginning of the real estate boom in 2000, and although I am bi-coastal, I have an apartment in New York, and spend a lot of time at my primary residence in New York, but I've taken advantage of the fact that in Los Angeles you can purchase vacant land for prices very often under a $100,000.00   I've built 5 houses in Los Angeles, and I've purchased 7 or 8 lots over these years, and every one of them (except for one) -- every one of these lots has been for less than a hundred thousand dollars -- and where else can you do that? What other major city can you buy a vacant lot and build a 2000 square foot house on the land that costs less than a hundred grand?

You tell me.

You cannot do it in New York City, that's for sure.

So the moral of the story is: because I met and became friends with one person in college, my whole destiny was transformed, and now I am able to say I do have money -- all because of that initial connection made when I drew the 2 of Spades, which led to my becoming friends with a guy from Beverly Hills, then spending time and living and working in California.

*****

Now I will give you an example of a person who changed my life after I graduated from Wharton

His name was also Stu, but this was big Stu.

Big Stu was my chiropractor. I met him through baby's mama.

Stu was a genius chiropractor! He's saved my life numerous times, when I've been in tremendous pain -- crack, crack, crack, bam! Fixed!

So one day I was getting an adjustment at Big Stu's boat; he had his chiropractic office on his boat in Marina Del Ray.

He said, "Would you like some raw milk?"

I said, "No thanks man, I don't do dairy."

"Why not?"

"It gives me mucus."

"Yeah, that's right, because pasteurized dairy will give you mucus -- but raw milk and raw dairy will not."

"Really?"

"Yeah, try it." So he gives me a cup of raw milk, and I drink the milk and say, "Hmmmm. Tastes like milk."

Stu says, "Yeah, but its raw and its good for you."

"What do you mean it's good for you?"

"Well, have you ever read We Want to Live Free from Disease by Aajonus Vanderplanitz?"

I said, "Who what where by what?"

He says, "Here, look at this book," and he gives me this pinkish purplish dog-eared hard cover book with a goofy guy smiling angelic-ly on the cover. So I look at the book, and it's a book about what is called Primal Nutrition.

I'm like, "Primal Nutrition, what is that?"

"It's the raw primal diet. It's eating food the way nature made it, not changing it with fire."

I flipped through the book and I came across this section called Remedies, and the Remedy that I happened to turn to that day was a remedy that said: "If your hair is thinning or if you're knees and legs feel weak like they're going to give out from underneath you, then you are suffering from a thyroid deficiency and you need to eat a lot of raw shellfish from the sea, such as oysters, clams and scallops." They are my favorite foods, and it just so happened that at the time my hair was starting to thin out. In fact, I'd been to a doctor not much prior to that to inquire about getting Propecia to combat my hair-loss. I ended up not doing it because it was expensive, but I still had this issue of thinning hair, and my legs were really bothering me, they felt weak, and my knees felt weak, and I thought, here is a remedy addressing two major concerns of mine, my thinning hair and my weak knees and legs, and all I have to do is eat my favorite foods in order to affect this remedy on myself. I want to know more about this!

So I said, "Can I borrow this book?"

He said, "I will sell you the book, it's $30 dollars, but if you're interested in it, you have to buy your own copy of this book."

I said, "Ok, I'll give you 30 bucks for this book."

So I gave him the $30 and I read the book in 24 hours.

I finished the book -- and it's a big fat hard cover -- and I soaked up that knowledge and information and I became a raw food primal diet eater.

And that completely changed my life.

Not only do I still have my hair (or most of it anyway,) but my legs are healed! Whereas, at one point I was forced to hold onto and brace myself completely on stair rails and banisters when I would walk down a flight of stairs (because my legs weren't strong enough to be able to walk down a flight of stairs without really supporting my weight on the handrails) to the point where now I can dance!

I can dance -- and I will say this with all due modesty: I'm a pretty damn good dancer!

But more importantly than that, I can walk. I can get

around. I don't really consider my legs to be a hindrance or an impediment to my success at living my life. They don't keep me from getting around in the world. If I need to go somewhere, I can walk -- it's no problem. And if I go to a nightclub with my beautiful wife, we can dance!

That little thing about eating the raw clams, oysters and scallops so that I could fix my hair loss and my knees -- well that ended up changing my whole entire career, because a big part of the raw primal diet is a product called raw butter. "Raw" means that the butter is not pasteurized, it's butter made from raw cream. They get the cream from the milk by putting whole milk in a separator, then they take the cream and put it in a churn, they spin that churn until the butter fat "breaks," and it becomes Butter.

At the time, there was a little problem in the raw primal diet community of Southern California: there was no raw butter.

Raw butter used to be made a long time ago by Alta Dena Dairy in Alta Dena, California, but somebody sued Alta Dena Dairy because they got sick (and I think somebody died from some contaminated raw milk.) So Alta Dena stopped making raw butter and all raw dairy products many years ago in California. And at that point in my little story, there was no raw butter available for sale in the United States.

After I finished reading the Primal Diet book I called Big Stu and I said, "Hey Big Stu, the book was great and I want to do the raw primal diet -- in fact I already started eating raw meat and raw eggs like it says, but so many of these remedies in the book include raw butter. What are we supposed to do?"

He said, "Yeah, there is no raw butter, but we do the best we can."

I said, "What do you mean we do the best we can? What do you do without raw butter? So many recipes call for raw butter."

He said, "Well, you use almond butter, and coconut cream instead."

"But is that an equivalent?"

He said, "Look man, do the best you can."

At that point in time I had this girlfriend named Natalia. So Natalia read the book she said "I want to do the raw diet too!" and we started eating raw meat with raw cheese, and she would cut it up thin like carpacio and pour on some olive oil, salt and pepper, and we'd have little primitive raw food dinners like that. But she said, "We need the butter. You have to find the butter, we need the butter!"

"Ok Natalia, I'll find the butter."

So I started calling up dairies, all around the country, and I would say, "My name is Clint and I'm looking for raw butter."

They would say, "What are you CRAZY!?!?!?!! What the hell do you want that for? Raw butter?! Who would want that? Why would anybody want that?!!!!!!!"

I'd try to explain, "You see, we're doing this raw diet, and a lot of people in my community are dying from Cancer and they are using raw nutrition to try to heal their bodies from cancer. So we need the raw butter because we want to live!"

Most of the time they would just hang up on me. "What are you, some kind of a whack job from California? Get out of here!"

157 phone calls later I found some lady who agreed to make me 40 pounds of raw butter. No joke. 157 phone calls later.

I gave her my whole spiel about the people trying to save themselves from Cancer, and somehow I convinced her. She agreed to do it on the condition that I paid in advance, and was charged twice as much for the un-pasteurized butter as she charged for regular pasteurized butter, and I said, "Great! I'll send you a money order, along with my FedEx account number, and would you put it in a box and FedEx it out to me?"

Sure enough, a couple of days later FedEx shows up with a big cardboard box, they dropped it off in the cockpit of my boat, I opened it up, and lo and behold, I've got 40 pounds of raw butter.

I am the only guy in California with raw butter!

I called up Big Stu and I said, "Guess what Big Stu."

He said, "What?"

"I've got 40 pounds of raw butter on my boat right now."

He said. "Get the fuck outta here."

I said, "Yup."

He said, "Bring me some."

I said, "Ok, I'll be right over."

So I take a pound of butter, I bring it over to Big Stu's boat, he takes a heaping spoonful of raw butter, pops it in his mouth and goes "Yummmm man that is good!"

I said, "Yep. That's raw butter. What do I do? I got 40 pounds of it."

"You could call my friend who's my partner in the raw milk

distributorship, and maybe he could buy it from you and sell it to some of his customers."

I said ok, he gave me the number, I called up his friend James, and that was the beginning of my butter career.

Pretty soon Big Stu was calling me the Butter Man. I'd call up Big Stu and he'd say, "Butter Man! How's it going Butter Man?"

And so that all progressed to the point where today, as President of the Five Star Butter Co., I am the Butter King of Las Vegas, and whenever I walk into the kitchen of a high end restaurant in Las Vegas I hear the same thing Big Stu used to say: "It's the Butter Man!" I've even been the Judge of Iron Chef America's "Battle Butter" (which was a show I proposed to the producers and made happen by sheer force of determination and will,) and I'm very happy and rewarded by my career in the Food Service Industry. And it's all because of my friendship and professional association with Big Stu.

*****

Earlier I talked about how sometimes you will meet people by accident, and other times you will set out to meet the person and they will change your life. That's exactly what happened with me and Tony Robbins.

I had read about and heard about Tony Robbins over the years, like everybody has. He's a pretty famous guy. About a year before I got into butter, I was living on my boat, I was driving a taxi on Friday and Saturday nights to pay the bills... I was at a pretty low point in my life, and I was surfing the internet one night when I came across Tony Robbins' Personal Power II.

I was so broke at that point that I maxed out my last credit card to pay $159 for the 30-day course on tape. I couldn't afford to buy the CDs I could only afford to get the tapes.

So I did the 30-day Personal Power Program and it started helping me. A couple months later I did the whole 30-day program again, which helped me some more, and eventually I started making money with my butter business and selling cream as well, and I got to the point that I could afford to attend the live "Unleash the Power Within" seminar with Tony Robbins teaching the course in person. And I'll tell you something, that course changed my life.

At that course I walked on fire with my bare feet.

I walked across a bed of burning coals.

From that experience I learned that you <u>can</u> do anything you set your mind to.

I remember the night before I attended the class, I flew to New York and stayed with my brother at his apartment in Manhattan. I was crashing on his living room floor the night before the course in a sleeping bag, thinking to myself What the hell have I gotten myself into? I could burn my feet tomorrow when I walk across those coals. What am I doing?

My brother and I drove out to the seminar location in New Jersey the next afternoon. Sure enough, the class starts at 5 o'clock pm, and at midnight they take us outside to go walk across the burning coals. 2500 people in a parking lot, and there's 10 rows of burning coals.

Tony teaches everyone to do their own "power move" -- you come up with your own personal move that's right for you. Mine is to stand there strong with my two feet planted firmly on the ground, my fists balled up next to my biceps, then I thrust them down by my sides in a very forceful downward motion and say YES!

So I go outside to the parking lot and see that Tony Robbins himself is up at the head of one of the lines of people walking across the coals, prepping them at the last minute and telling them when to walk across the fire. So I get on that line.

There I am waiting on line with Tony Robbins just a few feet away from me, the guy whose voice guided me and coached me and helped me for 30 straight days during his Personal Power II program that I listened faithfully to twice, and I am doing my power move, and everyone's doing their own power moves, and then there's a girl assisting Tony at the head of the line, and I get up to the girl by the head of the line and she goes "Okay, when I tell you to step up on the grass you step up on the grass and do your power move. Then Tony will tell you when to go."

Wow!

So exhilarating!

Tony Robbins is just a couple feet away from me.

I'm hearing him instructing people ahead of me, and it's his real voice, not amplified, not recorded – LIVE! Right there nearby!

Here I am, I've gone from a guy who could not really afford

to buy the cassette tapes for $159.00 to the point where now it is no problem for me to pay 800 bucks and go do the Tony Robbins seminar live with Tony Robbins, and there's Tony Robbins, the giant himself right there on the grass in front of me.

So the girl goes, "Okay, do your power move!" and I do the move and shout, "YES!"

"Okay, step up on the grass and Tony will tell you what to do!"

So I step up on the grass, and now I'm standing right next to Tony Robbins.

He says, "Do your power move!"

I do my power move and I shout, "YES!"

And he goes, "STRONGERRR!"

I do the power move stronger: "YESSSS!"

He goes, "GO!"

And now its time for me to walk barefoot across the burning coals.

I put out my right foot and I step down on the burning coals.

I can feel it's hot, but it does not burn my feet.

Step by step, I carefully walk across the burning coals in my bare feet, right down the middle of the glowing red embers.

I can feel the heat but its not burning my feet.

I get to the end of the coals and I step off the burning embers onto the grass and some people who are helping out have a hose and they wash my feet to make sure there's no embers stuck on the bottom of the soles of my feet, and I've done it!

I walked across the coals with my bare feet and I did not get burned.

From that experienced I learned that the human mind is capable of doing anything -- positively anything -- that you set your mind to.

The people that you meet in your life will be able to teach you these lessons, will be able to strengthen you or tear you down. Hopefully, they will be good for you -- but there's one thing that's for sure: people, are everything.

4

FOOD IS LIFE

I'm really excited to have you with me for this chapter because this chapter of this breakthrough project in my life (and hopefully in your life) deals with one of the most essential elements of success that I learned at the Wharton Business School. It's an element of success that anyone can take advantage of -- and everyone should be taking advantage of -- in their daily life, because this is something that you will be doing at least 2 or 3 times everyday.

This is an opportunity for you to be successful and to encourage success, to promote success in your life 2 to 3 times every single day. And everyone in the world is doing it too. What I am talking about, of course, is eating food.

When I grew up in New York City as a kid in the Urban Blight days of the 1970's, I was from a middle class family, and both my parents went out to work everyday. My mom's favorite joke was that she wanted to convert our kitchen into a closet. Not because we didn't have enough closet space in the house -- although there's never enough closets in an apartment in New York City -- but because she didn't like to cook. She didn't think it was worth her time and effort to put good food on the table for her family.

Now this is not a rail against dear old Mom (no resentment here, no of course not...) This is not about that.

What this is about is what I learned when I went to Wharton -- which was quite the opposite of what I learned at home.

What I learned at home was that food is not important.

What I learned at Wharton was that food is one of the most important things in the world, and by having a proper respect for food and by loving food and loving the social activity of eating with people, you can only do positive things for your life.

Let's begin with a very clear-cut example that I learned in my freshmen year at Wharton:

I was a struggling Calculus student.

I tell you, I had a <u>real</u> tough time with Calculus.

Low and behold, in the Spring I knew it was going to be tight, I was fighting for my GPA and I knew it was going to be really tough, and when around came the annual Take Your Teacher To Lunch Day, I jumped at that opportunity.

My professor was a huge bear of a man with a giant beard. He was from New Zealand, and when it came to be Take Your Teacher To Lunch Day, I tracked him down after class and said, "Hey Professor it's Take Your Teacher To Lunch Day, let me take you to lunch."

He look at me askance, like Why is this stupid kid wanting to take me to lunch? but said "Um… Sure."

I took him to Smokey Joe's, the classic campus bar and grille. We had burgers and draft Budweisers. I actually took a bite of the burger and crunched down into a piece of glass in the meat patty, but I didn't get cut, so I didn't let on that anything was wrong because I didn't want to make it a weird situation – that's how hard I was working this luncheon.

During that lunch, I was as "on" as I could possibly be, listening to every one of his stories and being as polite and engaging and interesting as I could possibly be. He told me about how he was skiing in Austria and broke his leg, and ended up having a great affair with the nurse in the hospital. And he told me about some of his research projects with calculus. And it was all Greek to me. Pretty much just like Calculus.

But by the end of that lunch it seemed like I was no longer just a number to that guy. I was a person.

A few weeks later, I took the final exam and ran into him on campus in a stairway as I was walking to some other class or to some other final. He looked at me and I said, "How did it go?"

He said, "You got the very last B in the entire class." There were like 400 people in that class and I got the very last B. Now was it only because I took him to lunch? Obviously not. Was there some discretion there on his part? Of course, there was. It became a choice between giving a B to some random number or giving the B to his young friend who took him to lunch --- and I got the B.

*****

Now I'll tell you a story that's even more important than my B in calculus: When I was a junior, I was in love with this girl named Wendy, and then I ended up getting my heart broken.

She wasn't into me nearly as much as I was into her, and it didn't work out, and I got pretty hurt.

Well one day a couple of months later I ran into her best friend, Nora, who was even more beautiful than Wendy.

Nora was a gorgeous blonde cutie-pie, and the sweetest person, and every guy was into Nora, but she was so beautiful and nice that no one would ask her out. I guess they were intimidated.

Well, I asked her to be my date for the Spring Formal at my fraternity. And I came up with the genius idea of making us dinner back in my apartment off campus after the formal was over.

So, I picked her up, we went to the fraternity, we danced, we had a great time, had a few cocktails, then we went back to my house and I prepared a rack of lamb.

Who the hell was I to be cooking a rack of lamb? I never cooked a rack of lamb before. But I looked up a recipe, I got some advice from a friend, I went for it, and man oh man did that rack of lamb set me up with one of the sweetest romances of my whole life!

It was just a perfect end to a perfect evening.

It could not have been more romantic and beautiful and it enabled me to begin a romance with one of the most beautiful and sweetest women I knew in my whole life.

Women love food. T hey may not want to eat it in front of you (if you're a man) all the time because they are trying to look skinny (or look like they are skinny or whatever) but women love food. Most people love food, and it's very important for every person to appreciate the importance of food.

"Food is life..." to quote my good friend and buddy from Wharton, John Favreau.

Food is life, and without food there is no life.

And the quality of the food that you eat is equal to the quality of love that you give yourself.

And it all begins with self-love.

There was a point in my life when I lost track of that. After college, I heard some guys in some pseudo-famous rock band talking on the radio about how all they ate was Burger King and Taco Bell, I was really into rebellion at the time, and I thought it was cool not to be into food.

I tell you something; that was the beginning of some of the roughest years of my entire life. The period of time when I was eating Top Ramen all the time. The period of time when I didn't even know what a good cut of steak was. A period of time when a Whopper was 99 cents and that was The Big Meal for me – a Whopper!

Those were some hard hard years. The years when I lost the importance of food were some of the lowest earning, most difficult, harshest times of my entire life.

And it was only (as I told you in the previous chapter) when I re-discovered the importance of food, when I re-emphasized the love that I gave to myself everyday and with every bite of food, by the act of putting good food into my body, that I was able to turn my life around.

Think about it like this: what kind of gasoline would you put into your beautiful BMW X5? I've got one, and I only use Super. I wouldn't dream of putting Regular Unleaded in my X5. I love that car, and I give it the best gas I can buy every time.

It's the exact same thing with food and your body.

Garbage-in, garbage-out. Great stuff in, great stuff out.

I'm not going to beat this dead horse. Just trust me on this. Eat the best food you can possibly get your hands on every single time. It sends a subtle message to your mind, and a very powerful message to every cell of your body, that you love yourself, that you're important, that the fuel you provide yourself is important, that you love life, and that you're playing this game of life to win.

ACTION ITEM: I want you to go to the best supermarket in your town and buy yourself a feast of amazing food. Take it home and set up the table with your best dishes and silverware, and when you prepare the food, do it with love and appreciation for how great it is. When you eat the food, I want you to take your time and really enjoy it. How does that feel?

5

GET THE MONEY!

Now we're going to be talking about a very important issue: Money.

Specifically we're going to talk about the value of a dollar.

This is one of the very first key concepts that you learn when you become a student at the Wharton Business School: a dollar today is worth more than a dollar tomorrow.

If I've got it today, that's worth more than if I'll get it tomorrow.

This is the basis of the entire financial industry.

A dollar today is worth more than a dollar tomorrow.

It brings in the issue of risk. How sure am I that I will actually get that dollar tomorrow? That's the basis of the entire banking industry and of our financial system.

This is where you get the concept of interest. Interest is the price that you put on the risk of getting your dollar tomorrow.

When you're a student at the Wharton Business School,

they talk about terms like the Net Present Value, what is that? Simple: What is the dollar tomorrow worth today? What is the dollar a year from now worth today? It's certainly not worth a dollar!

Getting a dollar a year from now, that's worth a whole lot less than a dollar today -- right now!

When you're in the Wharton School, the entire thing is a very intellectual exercise. And the amazing thing is that right from Day 1 they start out with questions like What is the Net Present Value (NPV) of $7,000,000.00 six years from now?

So you determine the interest rate based on the risk and you're supposed to calculate it back to find out that the Net Present Value of $7,000,000.00 in six years from now is X, whatever that may be.

I remember remarking to myself, Here we are 18 years old sitting, in E-con 101 talking about the net present value of $7,000,000 -- as if we're all going to be dealing with sums like $7,000,000. As if every kid in that class in E-Con 101 at Wharton would in his career be dealing with sums such as $7,000,000 … $20,000,000 … $150,000,000… This is the way you are programmed to naturally think in the Wharton Business School -- in terms of millions of dollars… Billions of dollars… You talk about trillions of dollars, you talk about GNP, GDP, gigantic sums of macro-economic significance, so that your brain is programmed to naturally think in giant numbers like that. It's part of the value that you get, and really for most of the graduates, it does become a reality.

In my junior year at Wharton, I setup an internship for myself at the Swiss Bank Corporation in New York City at the

World Trade Center, that was 1986. Got a job working for my high school wrestling coach, coach Mike, who was the Assistant Vice President at Swiss Bank Corporation those days, down at 4 World Trade Center. (That building was destroyed in the 9-11 attacks, by the way...)

By the end of the summer I was buying bonds for the Senior VP on the desk. I purchased $150,000,000 worth of Dai Ichi Kangyo Securities. I think he owned them for a grand total of 10 minutes, maybe half an hour, and then he sold them.

I didn't sell them, I only bought them, because I found them, he told me to buy them and I gave the order to buy them to the trader on the other end of the phone line, and there I was, 20 years old, and the training from Wharton had already come true. I was purchasing a bond for 50 million dollars and another one for 100 million dollars, these were bonds that were notes for the bearer to pay a sum in the future with implied interest rate all going right back to that simple concept: a dollar today is worth more than a dollar tomorrow.

It ended up not being such a great deal for that Vice President because the Dai Ichi Kangyo bank bonds were not very highly regarded, and the other traders made fun of him for buying them, because it was a mistake. So he bought them, and then a few minutes later he sold them. Maybe he lost $4000 on $150,000,000 trade.

But this was the key thing, one of the top 10 things that I learned at the Wharton Business School: a dollar today is worth more than a dollar tomorrow.

When I graduated Wharton, I learned the actual meaning of this axiom can vary in many ways, but it all comes back to the same issue how about how sure are you that you will get that dollar tomorrow?

Within just the past year I had an experience in my butter business with this exact issue. One of my clients called me up and said, "Hey Buddy, why don't you come over and pick up some of the money I owe you?"

I said, "I can't do it today. How about Thursday?" That would be 2 days later.

"Sure, sure, come on by, I'll be here."

Well, Thursday came and went, and he didn't answer his phone all day. I called him, a couple of times in the morning and once in the afternoon but I kept getting his voicemail. Then things piled up on my desk and I got busy for a week, now its 2 weeks later and I called him up again, "Blah blah blah," now he can't pay me right now.

A couple more weeks go by, I call him up, "I should be able to have most of the money for you the week after next."

"No problem, man." He's a good customer, and you can't sweat your good customers too hard for money. You have to be cool, and you have to make them feel like you trust them.

It was 6 ½ weeks later that I finally got the money.

Now, I knew the guy was good for the money, I've been doing business with him for a long time. But it just so happened that I had a lot of expenses in the intervening period, I'd been doing a lot of work around the house, cash got tight, and I ended up having to go in to my petty cash reserves to pay some workers! I had to reach into the pile! Just because that guy didn't get me the cash the day after tomorrow, the cash that I could have gotten if I had only gone over to see him that day when he called -- he didn't give me that cash for 6 ½ more weeks – do you see what I'm talking about here?

What if I had really been counting on that cash? I could have been! I mean, I could have needed that money for whatever reason; needed a new car, or needed to put down some money quick on a lot that was a quick sale by someone who needed to get money fast.

There are millions of reasons why I might have needed that money and didn't have it for 6 ½ weeks because I didn't get that dollar that day.

See in the real world, on Main Street -- not on Wall Street -- the value of a dollar today is even greater than the value of a dollar tomorrow because on Main Street, in the real world, you don't really know if you will be able to get that dollar tomorrow.

And that's why I have this motto: when someone offers to give you money, you go get it.

That's the exact same thing as a dollar today is worth more than a dollar tomorrow except its much more real.

When someone offers to give you money, get the money right then. "You want me to meet you at 4 o'clock on the corner of 3rd and Broadway? Ok I'll see you then." Want me to come to Venice to pick it up from you? Ok how is 4 o'clock?

Go get that money.

Get the money when you can get the money.

Its one of the first things they teach you at the Wharton Business School, but they dress it up, they call it the Net

Present Value of money, or they teach you that a dollar today is worth more than a dollar tomorrow.

All of it means the same damn thing: get the money -- NOW.

Get the money.

Go get that money now!

That's what they teach you in the Wharton Business School.

The basics are always very simple.

Setting goals, being liked, being good to yourself, getting the money.

ACTION ITEM: The next time somebody offers to give you some money, whatever amount that may be, large or small – I want you to make a point of getting that money as soon as possible. See what happens.

6

BE A WELL-ROUNDED PERSON

I've told you in a previous chapter that my educational at the Wharton School began when I was 14 years old and I read about the best business school in the world in a novel and determined right then I was going to attend.

The influence of the Wharton School began to shape and mold me into the man I am today right then when I was fourteen. And one of the most important lessons that I learned in my association with and education at Wharton was the concept of being a well rounded person.

This is something that is instrumental not just in your business career, but in every aspect of your life.

The first way that Wharton encourages well roundedness amongst its student body is by requiring it as a de-facto point of admission. Applicants are encouraged to demonstrate their diversity and well roundedness.

The student body is made up not just of the geeks who scored sixteen hundred on her SATs (I know that the standard is changed, but in those days the highest score you could get was sixteen hundred, and there were guys there who were in the statistics classes and in finance classes who had perfect scores on their SATs) super geniuses -- those guys were there. But by far and large, the majority of the student body was made up of people who were not just brains but were well-rounded people.

They were active in sports in high school, they were active in student government, they wrote for the newspaper...

In my case, I was an athlete on the New York City championship wrestling team (and a great wrestler, by the way,) I was an actor and singer performing the leads in many many school productions (I started when I was a little kid in 5th grade all the way through high school.) I was the business manager of the school newspaper and the treasurer of the student union, as well as holding jobs in my spare time. I had so many different jobs when I was a kid!) I also had diverse interests, I collect coins, I loved reading books, I loved music, attending concerts, investing in art) all of these things went into making me the well-rounded applicant that the admission board was looking for, and naturally (of course) they admitted me as an early decision candidate because Wharton was my first choice, I was so perfect, and a complete well-rounded scholar.

Then when I got to Wharton, one of the things I loved most about it was that you were permitted to take up to 50% of your classes in the other schools at the University of Pennsylvania.

Wharton is only one of the several colleges that make up the University of Pennsylvania (which was founded by Benjamin Franklin) and the student body at Wharton was permitted to take up to 50% of their classes outside of Wharton. So for example, I took oil painting, I took nutrition, I took playwriting, and I took creative writing...

I loved writing. In high school, my creative writing teacher was none other than the future- Pulitzer Prize winning author of **Angela's Ashes**, the illustrious, genius, funny, super-cool guy, Mr. Frank McCourt, and I always loved writing and taking his class for a year and a half. That really got the writing bug into me, and I've written many books and screenplays etc. Will talk more about that later but I continued to take writing classes in college, I took sociology, I took all kinds of classes that were not your typical Wharton finance or management or marketing classes, because the Wharton school wants its student body to be well-rounded, and that's how they encourage it.

*****

Since graduating, I would say that being a well-rounded person has been the most important part of my life, and has created for me not just a rich and rewarding and fun and fulfilling life, but also stability in these turbulent, volatile, and uncertain economic times.

As an entrepreneur, I have developed three different prongs of business activities, and I thank God for each one of those prongs because a three-legged stool is the most stable seat you can sit on.

In my case, over the years, the different arms of my business activities have varied in strength from time to time, so for example, before the food business really took off I had been writing books and screenplays and producing films and videos which I own all copyrights to, I own all marketing rights -- many of these products. And before the food business really kicked in, that was a major source of revenue for me and it continued to develop and become even more the source of revenue for me as things really started jelling for me in my late thirties.

Today the food business brings in more income for me than those intellectual-properties that I own. However, who knows what will be tomorrow as I deploy those assets in international markets, I expect that they will become renewed strong profit centers for me.

Over the past few years, during the real estate boom, building houses was a very profitable arm. Real estate development was a lot of fun and very profitable.

Despite the economic circumstances right now, with unbelievable levels of volatility in the markets and housing in the doldrums, despite all of that I do believe that people will want to retire to Costa Rica (where I am developing 14.8 acres) and will want to buy amazing houses in Los Angeles (where I am still developing properties) and so I will continue to put effort and energy and money and time into that leg of my three-legged stool of business.

But all the while, I'm reassured about the fact that I have the food services going strong, and that I am going to have income coming in from that and the intellectual properties, all because I'm a well-rounded businessman with diverse interests, diverse business interests and business capabilities, and all this was made possible because of the Wharton School's credo of developing well rounded graduates.

ACTION ITEM: Go out and sign up for a class or event that is completely out of the ordinary for you. Do something you've always wanted to do, but never had time for. Taking a cooking or dance class, go see a movie you wouldn't ordinarily be interested in, attend an opera or ballet, eat at a different ethnic restaurant than you ordinarily would. Expand who you are by being more well-rounded.

7

DRESS FOR SUCCESS

You may think it's a platitude to dress for success, but if it's such an obvious thing, then why does the Wharton Business Schools stress it so much? Why is it so important that it's actually something that I consider to be one of the Top 10 Things I Learned at The Wharton Business School? The school I paid a hundred thousand dollars to attend over four years back in the 1980's -- it took me four years of my time, sweat, effort, angst, blood and tears to make it through – and this is one of the most important things I learned: how vital it is to dress for success.

So first of all, what does it really mean to dress for success?

Does that mean that you have to wear a tuxedo? Well if you're a waiter in a fine restaurant, yes it does. But if you're a clown with Ringling Brothers & Barnum & Bailey Circus, wearing a tuxedo wouldn't be so appropriate, would it?

What if you were the Fire Marshall in the community, would wearing a tuxedo work? No.

Dressing for success is a completely context-based

endeavor. You have to dress for success in the context that you're operating in.

If you're working on Wall Street you've got to dress one way.

If you're working on Main Street you have to dress another way.

So how did this play out the Wharton Business School?

Number 1: just like I mentioned in several previous chapters, the Wharton Business School began shaping me with its dress for success credo before I ever even enrolled.

As I mentioned before, I went to my alumni interview when I was a senior in high school and I said that I put on my best preppy clothes. See, I wanted that interviewer to look at me as an obvious choice for admission to the Wharton Business School, so I dressed up the way the students at Wharton dress. I wore tan slacks, a button-down collar oxford shirt, and an argyle sweater vest with a pair of white Tretorn leather sneakers.

If you would've put me in a line up with a whole bunch of kids from the Wharton School you would not have been able to pick me out as the high school senior. I would've looked just like the rest of the students at Wharton.

Naturally, I was admitted Early Decision partially because I dressed the part in order to succeed.

*****

Now let's fast forward a little bit with the concept of

dressing for success to my experiences as a student in the Wharton School. Let's talk about freshmen year, Marketing 1.

I did not dress for success.

I forgot what I was doing when and I went to Marketing 1 classes wearing jeans and a polo shirt.

Now in all in all honesty, jeans and polo shirt is not something completely unseen on campus. Sure you're going to see students there wearing jeans and polo shirts... but not the ones getting the A's. The ones getting the top marks, the ones getting the A's, are dressing better.

How do I know that? Number 1: I didn't get an A in Marketing 1.

I think I got a B-.

More importantly, let's fast-forward to junior year when I did a specific experiment about dressing for success.

By junior year I had it all figured out: I had three classes that met on Tuesdays and Thursdays and I had two classes that met only on Wednesdays for three hours each.

I did a very profound experiment that year. To the Tuesday and Thursday classes, I wore a jacket and tie, sometimes I'd wear a suit, but at the very least I was always wearing a jacket and tie to each one of those classes, day in and day out. To the Wednesday classes, I just wore regular clothes generally Friday casual type clothes that you would wear to work on Friday casual if you work in a professional office, meaning no tie, no jacket.

You'd come into one of those Tuesday and Thursday classes and you scan the faces of students and you scan the overall appearance and clothing of the students, I would stand right out. You would say that I was undoubtedly the most together, put together, successful and professional looking student in those classes at the Wharton Business School, without a doubt.

So what do you think happened?

That's right, I got all A's in all those classes on Tuesdays and Thursdays; and for the Wednesday classes, one was pass-fail so I got a pass, and the other was a B.

From that moment forward, I knew that there was power in wearing a tie, that there's power in dressing for success.

Dressing like you care.

Dressing like you're on top of things.

Like you are on top of your world.

I know my daughter is a real fashion plate, so she's probably going to think, Oh well, Daddy, I don't need to pay attention to this so much because I'm quite the stylish dresser, but there's a key issue here and that's <u>appropriateness of attire.</u>

*****

Let's fast-forward now to a job I had a couple of years after graduating college. I went to work as a PA on big-budget studio feature film. At the time it was called Wings of the Apache (which I thought was an awesome title) and it was a movie starring Nicolas Cage, Tommy Lee Jones, and Sean Young, about the Apache attack helicopter pilots in an elite squadron of the United States Army. Ultimately the movie was released by the Walt Disney Corporation under the title

Firebirds. (Lame title, but what are you going to do?)

Anyway, I was a young whippersnapper in my first job in the motion picture industry, and I had a hell of a time in that job.

I thought I was going to get fired every day for the first two months because there was somebody on the team who really had it out for me. He hated me, and he did everything he could to make my life miserable, but nonetheless I persevered and managed to win the favor of one of my bosses who was the 2nd Assistant Director on the film (a really great guy who took me under his wing and started to teach me about how to do my job.)

Once I got good at it, I really started to like it. And I began to admire this Assistant Director and his boss the 1st Assistant Director.

Now the 1st Assistant Director on a movie, especially a big-budget movie like this one, is a major hardcore job. The guy who was doing that job was Matt Beasly, he was the 1st A.D., he was in his late forties and he was sharp -- a really sharp guy on top of everything -- running the entire huge site with hundreds of extras and helicopters and all kinds of stuff.

Matt Beasly was a real character, and he had a habit of wearing these really fun, cotton, button-down shirts with huge silly graphic images or patterns on them. They were kind of like Hawaiian shirts, but reinterpreted for the cutting edge Hollywood big budget studio feature film.

It was a very unusual look, and you could only get those shirts at expensive stores in LA like Fred Segal.

Well, when the production took off a couple of weeks for Christmas vacation and I went back to Los Angeles, I bought a number of those shirts at Fred Segal so that when I came back to the production in January looking like a junior version of Matt Beasly.

I wasn't wearing a jacket and tie, I wasn't wearing a suit, I was wearing the outfit of the man whose job I wanted to get.

Low and behold, we were a couple weeks into filming in January and Matt Beasly had to go out on some personal errand one day and there was the 2nd AD, J. P. promoted to 1st AD for the day, and there was me, stepped up to the position and job of 2nd AD.

Me! The guy who was almost fired off that movie so many times -- I never thought I would make it -- and here I was, the last PA standing, doing the job of the 2nd AD!

Was it only because I wore shirts like Matt Beasly? Definitely not.

My on the ball attitude, my willingness to get along with anyone, willingness to do whatever it would take -- that all played a part. But by wearing the same type of clothing as the big boss it sent a visual cue to the rest of the team that I was there to play ball, that I meant business, I wasn't screwing around.

I was wearing the uniform -- and here's the subtlety: dressing for success is a discipline, the clothes that you wear on the outside are representative of what's going on inside you.

A lot of people go about this unconsciously, and they just wear whatever they want to wear, whatever they feel like wearing. But to the astute observer, you will see that by wearing certain clothes on your body you can influence the way you feel on the inside.

So dressing for success can become a foregone conclusion, a self-fulfilling prophecy. Being the best dressed person in the room always works for you.

You can never over dress, but in order to really succeed, you've got to walk the finest line -- dressing as nicely as you possibly can without going too far.

Keep it in mind: if you want to succeed, you've got to wear The Uniform.

ACTION ITEM: This week I want you to try dressing up a bit more than usual. See if you notice any difference in the way people treat you, or in the way you feel about yourself.

8

FREE NEW MARKETING POWER

Yes folks, Marketing Power that is Free and New.

And you know what, marketing is everything -- so congratulations; you have found something very powerful and very valuable.

But before I get into the free new marketing power, I want to go into something that is basic and a foundational underpinning to a lot of these concepts in this book. I don't want to devote a whole chapter to the subject, I just want to touch on it right now and right here; and that is the issue of Quality.

Quality is a basic assumption. If you do not have an outstanding product, forget it. Nobody wants it. Nobody wants garbage, nobody want crap.

The only thing people want is something that is great, so if you don't have something great, don't even bother.

We try to get away with whatever we can get away – I know, and I can be as guilty of that sin as anyone if I don't keep up my guard and my personal disciplines, with but when it comes to the bottom line, in the long run, and in the end, it's got to be great or else don't even bother. If it's not great just go home, go to sleep and start again the next day because it ain't gonna work.

Now let's get into the Free New Marketing Power.

This is a concept straight out of Marketing 1 at the Wharton Business School.

The first day at Marketing 1 the professor talks about the most powerful words in marketing. It's a foreign concept for a lot of students. I know it was for me!

The class starts out with Stuart Debrucker, a full tenured professor, up in front of the class at the chalkboard. It's only 10:30 in the morning and he's already got <u>huge</u> sweat stains ringing the underarms of his white oxford button-down shirt.

Professor Debrucker says to the freshmen in Marketing 1: "You ever notice how you're walking down the street and you see a paper sign taped to a pole and it says 'Sex!' and then you look closer and it says 'Now that I've got your attention, I'm renting my one-bedroom apartment on 39th and Pine for eight hundred and fifty dollars'?"

Okay that's what we were talking about: Power Words.

The most powerful word in marketing is "Free." That's what everybody wants: something for nothing. You can't help it, it's a natural basic instinct of human beings to want something for nothing.

Therefore, if you give them something free, people want it.

It's free!

They can't help but want it!

It's free -- why shouldn't they have it?

Proctor and Gamble does this all the time: "FREE: 12 ounces in this package!" "Buy one get one Free!" "Buy 2 get 1 Free."

Philip Morris does that a lot: buy two packages of Camel Lights, get a third free. Buy three packages of Camel Lights, get this lighter for free.

Everybody wants something for FREE!

Next on the hit list is the word NEW.

After something free, the next best thing is something that's new!

Everybody wants something new.

New Tide.

The all new Chevy Malibu!

"…Another all-new episode of Nip/Tuck!"

New Coke for god sake! They got rid of the old Coke, Classic Coke, to go with New Coke!

Now it just so happened that it was a huge mistake -- but nonetheless, that shows you how powerful the word "new" is.

Coca-Cola Corporation, arguably the best marketing company in America, with the strongest brand in the world, ditched the reigning heavyweight champ of all brands to go with a "New" version of that brand.

A huge famous mistake, but nonetheless the greatest minds in marketing at the time made the decision. I would've done the same if I was in their shoes. If I was the executive in charge at Coca-Cola and you said to me, "Hey! We got an idea: we're gonna come up with New Coke!"

I would say, "Definitely! We are coming out with New Coke."

What I wouldn't have done is gotten rid of the old Coke. I would have kept Coke and just gone with New Coke in addition to the original brand. That's what I would have done.

And just the way they should never have gotten rid of Coke, they should never have ditched New Coke, either.

Personally, if I was in charge of the Coca-Cola Corporation, I would have brought back Classic Coke and just kept New Coke -- I mean why not? They already invested millions and millions of dollars in creating this brand.

I think the real stupidity of the whole New Coke fiasco was not keeping New Coke.

There had to be plenty of people who liked New Coke. There had to be hundreds of thousands people who loved New Coke -- they already spent the money, why get rid of it?

So Free New Marketing Power comes to you from the use of the words "free" and "new."

How does this play out at the Wharton Business School?

First of all, every year they don't admit old students into the Wharton school. No! They admit NEW students. Every year there is a new class that comes into the Wharton Business School. They don't bring the graduates back -- they are bringing in new students every year, "The All New Wharton Class of 2010!"

Second of all, when you hand in your case studies, when you hand in your tests, your little blue books (they give you these books you are to write your essays in for in-classroom tests, they call them the blue books, they are little tiny booklets with lined pages in them and have the University of Pennsylvania logo on the cover and a space for you to write your name and your class. Inside the book is where you write your essays when you're taking the test. Well every one of those books better be filled with new test answers because if was something that they already read in somebody else's test then you were going to get a call from Dean Stetson's office and questions from him like "Does this blue book contain your new work, or this is somebody else's old work?" They're not interested in anything old in there. That better be your brand-new test answers.

Every single blue book had better be filled up with new handwriting and answers!

Aside from that, they don't really get into it because what they're teaching you in most of these classes is how to manage multinational corporations how to tackle financial issues, and honestly they treat it as if it's so obvious that they don't even really stress it that much.

It was really once I graduated from Wharton that I began to understand the power of free and new

Let's take for example this book that you're reading right now. Chances are you have never met me, Clint Arthur, you never heard of me, you've never read any of my books or seen any my videos or films, you don't know me from Adam, and yet here you are reading the Free New Power book, and learning about free new marketing power.

I got you baby!

I got you!

I reached out into the bookstore aisle or into cyber-space by and I grabbed you by the most primal marketing instinct see you had, I grabbed you by your basic consumer instincts, I offer you something free and something new, and you dear reader, you could not resist. And don't be upset. You have been worked by the Wharton Business School's marketing principles.

You were like a deer in the headlights.

You are a victim of free new marketing power.

So you want free new marketing power? You need to go out and claim it.

You need to use the words free and new in your marketing.

Especially if you're an entrepreneur, especially if you're the little guy.

If Proctor & Gamble and Ford Motor Corp. and Coca-Cola marketing and bottling corporations are all using these words free and new, don't you think you should too?

Don't you think you deserve to use free and new?

You definitely do.

You owe it to yourself, to your wife, to your employees, you owe it to your suppliers who are counting on your business, you owe it to your kids who need to go to college-- you need to be using free and new.

All you have to do is reach out there and grab it.

Free new marketing power is now yours.

Congratulations! You may now go forth and conquer the

world.

ACTION ITEM: This week I want you to come up with 1 new idea that you can present to your clients, customers, or boss. When you do present it to them, stress the fact that this is something NEW, and notice the way they react to the idea of something being new. Do they pay more attention than normal? Do they lean forward or cock their head to listen more carefully? Have fun while you do this research and advance your career.

9

THE PRICE

In this chapter I'll be talking about a really really really interesting thing.

It's one of the most interesting things that I learned when I was a student at the best business school in the world: the Wharton School of Business.

Really, it's a shocking concept!

The concept is that there is only one price that you should be charging.

And really, there's only one kind of product you should be making to go along with your price -- at least according to the Wharton Business School.

You see, the price that the Wharton Business School teaches you to charge for your product or your service is a price that is High.

High price.

Then going along with that high price -- they actually teach you this at Wharton Business School -- you need to be charging a High Price for a High Quality product.

High price, high quality.

I learned this in the entrepreneurial management department of the Wharton Business School when I took The Game. (There was a class there given by Bob Aaronson, a legendary Professor at Wharton -- a legend! -- it's called The Game.)

When I took the Game, it was MBA students playing against college students. The game was they created a world in a computer model and they break up the class into corporations, teams of corporations, 4 students per team, and each team gets to choose their own name and they get to choose there own product and their own price and their own level of quality. Then they decide what they're going to do. How are they going to market that product?

Now one of the big lessons here is that once you determine your price and your quality, that's a great huge piece of your marketing right there. Price and Quality ARE marketing.

Your price, that is marketing.

Your level of quality is a huge component of your marketing.

In the game, the teams that won were the high price, high-quality teams.

I was not on one of those teams!

I had these altruistic visions of providing a good quality product at a cheaper price for the people.

I was going to have our company be like Volkswagen, the People's Car.

We lost.

You know who wins the game? Mercedes Benz wins the

game.

You know who wins the game? Whole Foods wins the game.

You know who wins the game? The New York Yankees win the game.

Rolex wins the game. Nike wins the game. Marlboro wins the game. Tide wins the game. These are the winners people!

The winners provide a <u>great</u> product, a truly high quality product that you can be passionate about, that you can rely on, that you can get excited about and tell your friends: "Look at my Rolex! Oh my God look what my husband gave me -- this Rolex is so beautiful!"

"Look at my Mercedes, I bought a Mercedes! I made it."

These are the products that provide something to aspire to, and then once you've achieved that goal you love the product.

You love it because it is great.

You love it because it meets your high expectations.

On an esoteric level, here you are spending 168 hours at work every week, you're working your ass off, you're working your life away. You leave the house every morning, you leave your beloved husband or wife at home with your little kid who you love, and you go out to the workplace and you spend your whole entire day away from your loved ones, away from your dog, away from backyard, away from your hammock in the sun, and what you do? You spend your whole day working like a dog, trying to make something out of your life, trying to get ahead, trying to accomplish something so that you can retire one day and be able to send your kids to college so that they can make it and have a better chance than you had, so that their lives will be better than yours.

You spend all that time, five, six, seven days a week working like an animal to make it.

Well, if you're going to spend that huge chunk of your life, if you're going to spend all of that time -- and really all you've got is time -- shouldn't you at least dedicate all that effort and time to something that is truly great?

What's the point otherwise?

What's it worth if there you are, lying on your deathbed, and a reporter comes in to interview you. They say, "What was your life about?"

"Well, I worked my whole life, dedicated my life to my work, got up every day to work, got on the phone made the cold calls, push the pencil, shipped the product, got a speeding ticket because I was trying to get to FedEx in time…"

Then the reporter will ask you, "What were you working so hard to do?"

"Well, I was making this mediocre product. You probably never heard of it…"

What's the point of that?

If you're going to work like an animal, if you're going to give up all your time, at least do something that is worthwhile.

At least create something, dedicate your life to something that really is quality.

It's really the only chance you've got.

The marketplace doesn't give a shit about another mediocre product. There are a million mediocre products out there, and nobody can care less.

What the marketplace will allow is an outstanding product to succeed.

It better be outstanding.

I tell you, it absolutely better be outstanding.

You go to any of my client restaurants in Las Vegas, go to Picasso, you go to the Le Cirque, you go to Aureole, you go to Alex Strata's restaurant at the Wynn, you go to this Nero's steakhouse at Caesars Palace, go to Bobby Flay's restaurant Mesa, you taste the butter you tell me that butter's not outstanding.

Let me tell you something: if that butter wasn't freaking phenomenal it wouldn't be there. They would just be using the same crap that everybody else is, and paying regular prices for regular butter -- but no! I offer them an outstanding product.

So outstanding that I took over the whole Bellagio, I'm taking over Caesar's Palace... I've got the best restaurants all over town using my butter.

Why?

Because it's outstanding.

It is a high quality product.

Now, the trick is to find the high price that's high enough so that you're making money, but not too high that people can't afford it. That's the real trick.

Notice I didn't say that Ferrari was the brand to emulate.

I didn't say that Bentley or Rolls Royce were the brands to emulate. Those are little tiny specialty niche brands.

There's a lot of pride in being Ferrari -- you talk to my friend Mimmo, and if Mimmo could be Ferrari he would die and go to heaven! He would cut off his left arm if he could say, "I own Ferrari!"

But Ferrari is not taking over the world. You only see a Ferrari every couple weeks driving on the streets in LA. You see Mercedes-Benz driving on the road every day. There is one parked out in front of my house right now -- and I don't live in a rich neighborhood, either. One of my neighbors has one of those Mercedes C-Class sedans parked right in front of my house right now.

They're everywhere!

They are taking over the world!

They are high price, high quality machines, and they are the leaders in their marketplace.

That's what you want to be.

Not just because it's smart.

Not just because Wharton Business School teaches you to do it. But because that's the only thing worth spending your time on.

So, when you're creating your product, when you're creating your position in the marketplace, when you're thinking What am I going to do with my job? Where do I want to work? Do I want to work for Volkswagen, or do I want to work for Mercedes? The answer is clear.

The only price endorsed by the Wharton Business School and by me is high price, high quality.

10

CUSTOMIZE FOR CUSTOMERS

Welcome to Chapter 10, and congratulations to you for joining me here, because this topic is a mega topic: Customize for Customers.

I am not talking about Customizing for Customers that you already have.

I am talking about Customizing to get Customers.

Period.

You want customers? You gotta Customize!

People want what they want, and it varies.

Gone are the days when you could have Model T in any color you wanted it as long as it was Black.

In the 21st Century, you've got to make a different pair of Nikes for every single customer if that's what it takes. That's why Nike has online custom designed sneakers that you can buy and have sent to you.

How does this play out with regard to the Wharton Business School?

First of all, as I've stated in previous chapters, this idea of Customizing for Customer worked its way into my life before I was ever a student at the Wharton Business School.

My product was my candidacy to become a student at the Wharton Business School.

I was the product.

And I customized my product.

I customized myself into the student that the Wharton Business School wanted.

I created it.

They wanted 1300+ on the SATs, I scored 1300+ on the SATs.

They wanted certain scores on achievement tests, I got those scores.

They wanted a certain Grade Point Average, I got that.

They wanted well-rounded academic and extracurricular activities, I did that.

They wanted the students to look a certain way, that's the way I looked.

They wanted a particular kind of essay, well written, intelligent, from the heart. That's what I gave.

I gave them the custom product that they required so that they could approve the purchase order -- which was my admission into Wharton Business School as an early decision candidate.

Continuing in the University of Pennsylvania at the Wharton Business School I continued to customize my product for the customer. In particular, I'm reminded of this one class I had which was taught by freaking Communist.

As I stated, you had to take a certain amount of courses out of the Wharton School, which is one the things I loved about it. Now one of the courses that I took outside the Wharton School was to fulfill the diversification requirements of the school. I had to take a couple of sociology classes, and I don't remember what the name of this class was, but I do remember that the teacher was a woman and that she was a Communist.

If you didn't spit back the answers to her test and her take home exams in Communist language, I swear to God, if you didn't talk about The Workers and the unjust treatment of the Workers by Management, if you didn't tow the proletariat party line, you didn't get an A.

So here I am, a budding young Capitalist, majoring in entrepreneurship at the Wharton Business School at the University of Pennsylvania, the best business in the world, the bastion of capitalism, and I had to customize my product for the customer by making my answers sound like I was a freaking Communist, and you know what -- that's exactly what I did. That's what she wanted, that's what she got.

See I wasn't going to the Wharton Business School to get Cs and Ds -- that wasn't the point of going to the Wharton Business School!

The point of going to the Wharton Business School was to be successful, was to have high GPA, to be an excellent student at the Wharton Business School.

I was not going to let some Communist teacher screw me up just because of the types of words that she required.

That was the class, the class taught X Y Z, and if you wanted to succeed in that class, you had to demonstrate that you mastered the material in the class using the language of the class. You had to conform to the social requirements of the class in order to succeed.

I talked about dressing for success in a previous chapter; in this case I dressed my answers for success in the appropriate costume and garb for the circumstances, which was Communist lingo.

*****

Now lets fast-forward to after the Wharton Business School. How has this idea affected my career, my business, my money?

This idea of customize for customers is the foundation of my entire Five Star Butter Company business.

I remember it very clearly when it all began.

I kept going back to Le Cirque restaurant at Bellagio, every 6 months I'd go in there with my little tub of butter, fresh off the farm in Kansas. I showed the butter to the chef and he'd say, "Man, I love this butter!" (Actually, he said it in French, but for the sake of everyone being able to understand it right now, I assume not everyone understands fluent French, as I do, so I just say it in English and he'd say) "Man, I love this butter, but I need the shape! What about the shape? Do you have the shapes, Clint?

"No I don't have any shapes. This is all I've got."

After the third trip into Le Cirque -- can you imagine slogging through the desert of Nevada with a cooler full of butter, it's a hundred degrees out and everybody keeps saying

"No"?

After that third trip into Le Cirque, chef Mark Poidevin is having lunch with his other chefs. There's these 10 chefs in white chefs coats and aprons sitting around this long table in the main dining room at Le Cirque, its all plush velvet, purple, all kinds of fancy silk on the walls, gaudy and extravagant colors, its the most lavish and impressive luxury dining room that I've ever been in. I said "Hey guys, you want some butter for your lunch?"

They go "Wow! Oh yeah man! Thank you! Fantastic, delicious!" But then he goes, "But what about the shapes?"

I said, "What shapes are you talking about?"

He says, "You know we have this special shape, it says Le Cirque."

I said, "Show me the shape."

He takes me down to the walk-in cooler, he pulls out a box, and in the box is a piece of butter. It doesn't look like my butter. This butter is in the shape of an oval, and on the butter stamped right on the butter it says Le Cirque. That's the name of this restaurant.

I said, "Let me see that box." I grab the box, then I looked at the name of the company on the box, and I said "Alright, thank you chef. I'm going to find out if they will put my butter in your shape. If I can put my butter in your shape, do you want it?"

He said, "Oh yeah, definitely."

So I call up the company and get the company to put my butter in the Le Cirque shape. I call him back: "I got the butter in the shape."

"Great!"

That was the beginning of what is now an empire.

My kingdom, Las Vegas.

My domain, Custom Gourmet Butter.

Giving the chefs exactly what they want.

They want .75% salt, that's what they get.

They want 2% sea salt from France, that's what they get.

They want it in a shape that weighs .6 ounces, that's what they get.

They want .4 ounces, that's what they get.

They get custom products.

They get exactly what they want.

What is my job? To give the chefs <u>exactly</u> what they want.

You know why? If you don't give them exactly what they want in terms of quality, price, the delivery specification, frequency, minimum orders -- if you don't give them <u>everything</u> that they want, then they'll just get it from the next guy, or they'll just continue to use the vendor that they already use, to buy a product that they're familiar with, that is close to what they want but they already know what it is, so they just keep on using it.

This idea of customize for the customer -- if you can embrace that, if you can give people exactly what they want instead of what you want to sell them, you will be amazed at what will happen to your business.

11

THE SECRET WEAPON OF
THE WHARTON SCHOOL

Chapter 11 is the killer of all killers.

This is the lesson that I learned at the Wharton Business School that is more valuable than anything you may have learned or picked up or been told or stumbled upon in your whole life.

I don't care what it is you may know, or who told it to you -- this is more powerful.

With this magical power you can do anything.

You can befriend anyone.

You can sell to anyone.

You can achieve anything you want.

So what is this magical power?

It's so simple that I taught it to my daughter when she was 5 years old.

Quite simply, it is called "Assume the Rapport."

What does that mean? It means if you want to be

somebody's friend, just act like you already are their friend. That's how I explained it to my five year-old daughter, and I think it's really the best way.

Of course you can complicate it, you can make it more "sophisticated" by using dressier words, but at its core that is it.

Want to be somebody's friend? Just act like you're already their friend.

The hardest this thing about this is doing it.

It sounds so simple -- I know!

But do it?

Go ahead have the conviction to do it!

My friend, if you can do it, you could become the next Barack Obama, because from where I've been sitting, that guy just assumed that he was the next President of the United States, and look at him! He assumed that rapport with the United States of America and the whole world. Look at all the hundreds of thousands of people that showed up in Berlin, Germany to hear that guy talk.

So how did this work its way into my curriculum when I was a student at the best business school in the world?

It started out very innocently. I had heard about this fraternity, it was supposedly the coolest fraternity on the whole campus -- if not, in all of America. They had parties there that were the legendary! When I went to go visit Penn, I spent the night sleeping on the floor of a guy who went to Stuyvesant High School, he was a year ahead of me and I had known him when I was on the gymnastics team. He mentioned these parties at The Castle. "Those parties are really cool, but it's just really hard to get in to those parties, and so I don't really go." That's what he said.

The place looked like a castle, it's made out of blue-gray limestone, built in the late 1800's, they have legendary parties, they were located in the absolute center of campus directly adjacent to Steinberg Dietrich Hall (which is or was the main building of the Wharton Business School) and if you get into The Castle then you live in The Castle, so I could basically roll out of bed and go to classes right next door at the Wharton Business School.

Sounded good to me!

Oh, and by the way -- you know that guy Steinberg (as in Steinberg Dietrich Hall, the one who gave all the money to build the building that housed the Wharton Business School) his son was in The Castle! He ended up being one of my business partners -- but that's a whole another story.

So I show up for freshman orientation and we have a little get-together in the dorm, so I quickly befriended this fellow Wharton student, he lived directly across the hallway from me. His name was John Favreau, he was from Feeding Hills, Massachusetts, he was obviously very smart, well brought-up, very presentable young man, and he and I hit it off immediately.

I told him about The Castle, and he said yeah he had heard about it too. We both wanted to get in.

So we go to up to The Castle, walk up the stone steps to these huge wood and glass front doors with brass handles, dark stained old wood, and we ring the bell.

This very boppy young man, very preppy, with a short military haircut answers the door and introduces himself as Brian Hanstien, President of The Castle. Would we like a tour? We'd love a tour!

We talked to that guy very casually, friendly, told them that we were interested, we loved the house, we really appreciated his time, everything was cool, the pictures on the wall of all the old brothers from the 1920's and 30's and 40's and 50's 60's 70's are all cool, and we went back to our dorm, we bought him a bottle of Bombay Sapphire Gin, got the prettiest girl on our hallway to bring it over with a note, "Thanks for the tour! Very truly, John Favreau and Clint Arthur."

The entire "rush" process went on for us just like that, simple and easy. We went to cocktail parties there which were "coat & tie" -- we dressed in jackets and ties. We held our liquor well! This was an important thing because there were a lot of cocktail parties, and I remember asking the Rush Chairman, a very tall preppy young man named Ed Daley, "Any advice for a young freshman who wants to become a brother of The Castle?"

Ed Daley looks down at me very seriously and deadpans, "Drink heavily!"

So we went to all the cocktail parties, we looked the part, we spoke the part, we drank the part, and low and behold, we just assumed our away right into the freshman class of pledges at The Castle.

It was that simple.

As a result of being a brother at The Castle, not only did I live in the house and have all those amazing experiences of jacket and tie dinners every Sunday night, and being brothers with all these really cool men, having all those parties right in my home, having the social training of being part of a brotherhood like that. But I also made some of my very best and closest friends in the world -- even to this day -- who were brothers of The Castle. And I would have to say that assuming the rapport has really shaped my life.

I use it all the time in business.

Whenever I go in for a sales call, you know I'm assuming the rapport.

That prospect <u>is</u> one of my clients; someone whom I look out for, take care of, I provide them with a precious product and I hold their interest as my own. I assume all that going in.

Use that power in your everyday life!

You want to be somebody's friend, just assume the rapport.

ACTION ITEM: I want you to go out into the world right now and use this piece of technology. That's right, go up to some total stranger and just assume the rapport of being their friend. Don't be psycho about it! Just be cool, be friendly, strike up a nice conversation, and initiate a new friendship with somebody. Chances are very likely that you will make a new friend. This works! Have fun with it!

12

WHAT <u>REALLY</u> MATTERS

Welcome back to another all-powerful chapter of for your career and business – and for your life! This section of the book is going to teach you what <u>really</u> matters.

You see, there are a lot of people out there who want to try and convince you that they know what matters.

They will try to make you believe that "Quality is Job One."

That price is the bottom line.

That the name is what makes the difference.

That marketing is all that matters.

That management is what rules the day.

That 6 Sigma, or X Y Z is the way to be.

Folks, I'm here to tell you something completely different.

I'm here to tell you what I learned at the Wharton Business School... What the professors taught me during my 4-year education at the best business school in the world.

Do you want to know what really matters?

Do you want to know what will make your business

recession proof? What will protect you during the current times of economic uncertainty or any period of economic turmoil or upheaval?

What will keep you employed and doing business day after day regardless of what your competitors do, and regardless of circumstances?

The answer is very simple.

It is a single word,

And that word is "Everything."

That's right, Everything is what matters most.

That's what I learned at the Wharton Business School.

How did I to learn that? Is there a class at the Wharton Business School called "Everything Matters in Business 101"?

Not exactly.

First of all, this lesson began to be instilled in me by Wharton before I ever even set foot on the campus of the Wharton Business School.

It began that day when I was fourteen years old and I decided that I was going to the Wharton Business School and I started to mold myself into that type of candidate who would be accepted by the Admissions Department.

I read up about the Wharton Business School.

I looked at the profile of successful candidates who gained admission. And what did I learn?

I learned that those candidates had everything going for them. SAT's, Achievement Tests, GPA, Advanced Placement classes, extracurriculars, sports, letters of recommendation, and the personal interview. It all had to be World Class, top-notch, of the highest caliber.

So that's what I did. I created myself into that candidate, with everything everything everything that they wanted.

Next, when is actually a student at the Wharton Business School, one day I had a meeting at my professor's home. His name was Myles Bass and he was an entrepreneurial genius.

The class was entrepreneurial management, and I was an A student.

One day he invited me to his home, and I showed up in my customary suit and tie, because at that point (when I was a senior) I was wearing a suit and tie at every class I attended (except Oil Painting.)

So I arrived at his understated house in a very upscale neighborhood, and ring the front doorbell. 30 seconds later the door swings open and there's Myles Bass standing there dressed in a bathrobe. He takes in everything about me in the moment of a smile and said, "Are we going to the same meeting here?"

So I chuckled and loosened my tie. (As a side note, if you're going to a meeting at guy's house on a Saturday morning, you probably shouldn't wear a suit and tie. Probably somewhere between a bathrobe and a suit will work fine! PS: I did take a meeting with a client at a resort where I was vacationing, so naturally I showed up in a bathrobe, which worked out to be fantastic!)

But anyway, back in Cherry Hill, New Jersey, in the spring of 1987, we sat down, I loosened my tie, and Myles said to me,

"You know I'm looking at you, and I'm noticing everything about you. I notice if you bite your nails, I notice if you smoke cigarettes -- and by the way, successful men and women in business don't smoke cigarettes. I notice if your shoes are shined or if you've got a ketchup stain on your tie. I notice everything, and you don't want anything to distract me ... when we're in our business meeting ... from your objective."

So everything has to be perfect.

Thank you, Miles.

There's a reason why so many students in the Entrepreneurial Management major – including me – loved you and thought of you as their favorite professor.

Now fast-forward to the real world and the 21st Century, where the tests come not once a week or once every semester but every day, 24/7 and 365.

The test comes on the loading dock. If your delivery guy curses out the Receiver, you're liable to lose that client.

The test comes in the walk-in when the QC Inspector looks at the product -- if it's not the right temperature when it arrives, they're going to refuse it.

The test comes when the customer tries the product or uses the product. If it's not perfect, you fail.

The test comes when your Invoice arrives. If it's not correct it's not going to get paid.

The test comes when FedEx comes to pickup the product to ship it to the client. If the bill of lading or air bill is not correctly filled-out, its not going to get delivered properly, and then there's going to be a delay, and then you're going to lose the client.

The test comes when your competition walks into the purchasing department and tries to undercut your price. If your product doesn't have the quality, the delivery history, the right pricing, you're going to lose to your competitor.

The test comes every day.

And what is the test? The test is on everything.

Everything, everything, everything matters.

A few years ago -- that would be about eighteen years after I graduated from the Wharton Business School -- I took a leadership seminar, it was called Basic Leadership Training. You know what the mantra was? You know what they drilled into your head every day of the seminar for six weeks? Everything, everything, everything matters.

So that's why, when I'm at the gas station filling up my tank with Super Unleaded, when I go over to the squeegee rack and pick up the squeegee to wash my windshield, I also pick up the paper towels. Because I have to make sure that every inch of that windshield is perfect.

Why? Because everything matters.

ACTION ITEM: I want you to use extra care and diligence in all the small little details of what you do today, and repeat the mantra "Everything, everything, everything!" See how this little tiny shift in your perception of quality makes a difference in your life this week. If it does, I want you to keep it up as a daily practice to make yourself a better person.

13

$1000 GOLDEN NUGGETS

Here are 9 gems of wisdom that I learned at Wharton Business School. Each one is probably worth at least $1000.00, but I don't feel that any of them is enough to devote an entire chapter to, so I've assembled them here as Golden Nuggets. In all, this chapter has a Golden Nugget value far in excess of $9,000.00

$1000 Golden Nugget #1
Work Smart, Not Hard.

We had a guest lecturer in Myles Bass' Entrepreneurial Management class who was actually my very good-friend Hillary Frankel's father. His name was Stuart Frankel, and he was a really really really really really successful stockbroker on Wall Street during the booming 1980's market. Stewie was a guy you would never have heard of, but a guy who all the really huge investors would go to when they wanted to trade large blocks of stock on the Down Low. His clients were Ginormous guys like Ivan Boesky. They didn't want people to know that they were buying a certain stock because then the stock would get bid up. So they would go to Stewie, and Stewie would buy the stuff for them quietly.

I remember he kept repeating over and over, "Work smart, not hard."

What does that mean?

It means, don't do it yourself if you can delegate it to somebody else to do.

Or, if you can do something in less time, with less money, and less stress – then do it that way!

It means, Use Technology to leverage your time and power.

It means, Make sure you're talking to the Decision Maker.

It means, Outsourcing...

Sticking Close To Home...

Choosing Work That You're Good At...

Leveraging Your Network...

Investing in The Future...

It means anything that you can do to reduce your effort, decrease your costs, reduce your time – anything that will let you be more FREE.

This was a big deal.

It went against the old Puritanical work ethic that used to be prevalent in our country: that you have to work hard to get ahead or to make it. I heard it a million times when I was growing up. "You have to work hard to make it! You have to work hard to get ahead in this world." That's what my dad used to say all the time.

But the Wharton School taught me that if you can work smart instead of hard, then that's much much better.

Here's the best story about working smart instead of hard: In my Senior year I was taking a class in the Entrepreneurial Management Department called "Mergers and Acquisitions." The final exam was a take-home test on the Borroughs-Sperry Merger, which combined two huge computer companies into a new corporation called UNISYS. At the time, it was the largest computer industry merger in history, and made UNISYS the second largest computer company with annual revenue of $10.5 billion, and 120,000 employees.

A kid from the class named Alex Moscovitz called me up one evening a few days before the test was due, and was nice enough to include me in the smartest idea I ever heard.

He said, "Dude, the President of UNISYS Corporation is speaking in Vance Hall tomorrow afternoon, I'm putting together a group of students from our class, we're each going to ask him a question about the merger from our final exam, and like that we'll have all the answers for the final straight from the horse's mouth."

Now THAT was truly working smart.

And that's exactly what we did.

I think there were five of us, four guys and a girl, and each of us answered every question on the M&A Final Exam about the UNISYS merger like this, "According to Joe Shmo, President of UNISYS, the answer to this question is...."

We all got A's.

$1000 Golden Nugget #2

Never Make a Sideways Move in Business

That counts if you are on the corporate ladder, and it also if you're a businessman or an entrepreneur.

You don't want to take a job at another company just because you're going to make a few thousand dollars more. You'll get a reputation as a guy who's not loyal, who's ready to jump ship.

Likewise, you don't want to switch suppliers or vendors just to save 20¢ a pound. You want to make a move that makes a big difference, a move that takes you up or down the ladder, either on the career ladder or on the supply ladder. Vertical Integration is good, but switching suppliers is generally lame.

A few years ago I contemplated switching my source for putting my butter into the shapes my clients need. I shopped around with the other companies who do that work, and I realized I'd only be saving a few pennies per pound by switching to another company. Now granted, with all the many thousands of pounds of butter I sell every year, that would have resulted in a savings of several thousand dollars.

But I got good service from my supplier, and I believe that companies have the potential to recognize and reward loyalty. Especially if they're smart.

It doesn't always happen, but it should happen.

I try to reward my clients who are good clients by going above and beyond the call of duty with Service. When they need same day delivery, I give them Same Day Delivery and I don't charge them for the rush. They can call me any day of the week and I will answer my phone for them. They know that if they need me, or if they need something special, or if they need me to make something out of the ordinary happen for them, that I am available.

You want to build relationships with clients and suppliers, and to stay in those relationships for long periods of time.

To that end, it is very important that you become a person or company that is not thought of as a "cheapskate", digging for every last penny in a negotiation -- because that is evidence of your not understanding the value of relationships – understanding that relationships will save your ass.

$1000 Golden Nugget # 3
The Triple-It Rule

Yup, that's what is called, The Triple-It Rule.

This was an actual question on Myles Bass' Entrepreneurial Management class Final Exam: "Explain The Triple It Rule."

The Triple-It Rule is very simple: However much time you think a project is going to take, and however much money you think it's going to cost, triple it. That's The Triple-It Rule.

That's what it's <u>really</u> going to cost.

That's what it's <u>really</u> going to take.

It's going to take 3 times as much time.

And it's going to cost 3 times as much money.

That is direct from the Wharton Business School.

You will ignore the Triple-It Rule at your own peril.

There will always be cost overruns.

There will always be delays.

There will always be something unexpected to slow you down or take a bite out of your wallet.

If you're really really really really good at what you do, maybe you will get away with only a Double-It. But most people, and especially most start-up entrepreneurs will find themselves falling victim to this inescapable axiom – and you better have the cash cushion and the extra time built into your schedule to go with the flow.

Or else you will be out of business…

Before you even get started…

Because of your failure to heed The Triple-It Rule.

$1000 #4

Shake With A Firm Grip

I remember when I was a brother in The Castle, we had this kid who was trying to become a pledge, and when you shook his hand it was like shaking hands with a dead fish. We all made tremendous fun of that guy.

I don't think he got in <u>because of his handshake</u>!

At the same time, I've met several women who shook my hand with an awesome firm grip, and I always make note of it, I always compliment them on their handshake, and I always make it a point to speak with them and to pay attention to what they have to say. So ladies, it's especially useful for you to have a firm handshake. It will get you noticed, and it will create opportunities for you throughout your life. How's that for a little nugget of free new power? Just something as simple as a firm handshake – it's going to do so much for you!

$1000 Golden Nugget #5
Be Who You Are

Water finds its own level so you can't pretend to be somebody that you're not, it just won't go over.

Even more importantly, when you get to the end of the day, you're just going to end up where you belong anyway.

It was very interesting: I thought The Castle was a very WASPy blue-blood fraternity. The when I got in, I realized it was full of guys just like me -- and I am not a WASP, and I am not a blue-blood.

So it was really interesting to see what was real versus what I thought it was.

It ended up that I was just where I belonged.

$1000 Golden Nugget #6
Use Your Full Name

You shouldn't say, "Hey, my name is Matt."

You should say, "My name is Matthew Bledsoe."

Imagine Tony Robbins; would Tony Robbins ever call you up and say "Hey its Tony!"?

No! Tony Robbins would never call you up and say "Hey it's Tony!"

He would say: "Hi, this is Tony Robbins!"

Maybe if you were his wife he would just say something casual like, "Hey Baby, it's me," or "Hey baby." But to the World At Large, Tony Robbins is always going to say, "This is Tony Robbins."

And you should always use your full name too.

It sounds much more impressive, especially when you're calling for dinner reservations. You call up the restaurant and say, "Hi this is John Smith calling, and I'd like a reservation at 7PM." It makes people think that you are much more important if you use your full name.

$1000 Golden Nugget #7
Be Social

When you're at a party, meet people.

Go up to people and say Hello! Where are you from? What's your name? And when they say their name, you're going to forget it -- because we all have that tendency to think about ourselves when meeting new people; Am I looking good? Am I making a good impression? -- So when people tell us their name we generally forget it. Don't be afraid later on in the conversation to say, "I'm sorry, what was your name again?" It's much better to know their name than not.

If you know their name then you've actually met somebody.

If you don't know their name, then next month you'll be trying to remember who they were and you'll be like "Hey, remember that guy I was talking to at that party 3 weeks ago? Do you know what his name was?"

Don't let that happen!

Say to the person: "Tell me your name again so I can remember you."

$1000 Golden Nugget #8
Don't Be A Snob

Most things are not what they seem.

Most snobbery is based on fallacy; it's based on wrong ideas and misunderstandings. It's just not worth it to be a snob.

My recommendation is that you have an open mind. That you don't think you're better than anyone or anything or any place.

Just be open, and not a snob.

I'll give you a terrific example of how being a snob worked against me in a major way: after I graduated from college I moved out to Los Angeles and started hanging out with my friends and fraternity brothers who were from California.

My best friends from college grew up in Beverly Hills, and they had a lot of snobbery about The Valley, about living in The Valley, and about people from The Valley, so naturally I adopted those snobbish attitudes myself and became a very snobby West-sider.

Fast-forward to one morning in The Valley about eight years ago, I took my little daughter to a private school interview and I was killing some time until the interview was over, so I went into a Verizon store to see about a new case for my Motorola Flip Phone.

When I came out of the store I saw my future wife crossing the parking lot, so I followed her into the store, started talking to her, then I started dating her, and after a few months we were living together in her house in The Valley.

And as I got to know The Valley, I got to love The Valley.

First of all, there's less traffic there. That aspect alone in Los Angeles is well worth emphasizing. Then there's less cops trying to give you speeding tickets, there's less competition for parking, and everything is less expensive than on the West Side. Everything! Food, clothes, entertainment, everything costs less.

In addition, Real Estate opportunities in The Valley are abundant. The ground is flat there, so it's easier to build. And best of all, it's almost always summer in the valley – nine or ten months a year, it's 80 degrees and sunny in The Valley!

And I don't know about you, but summer is my favorite time of year.

Today, if you ask my opinion about where's the best place to live in Los Angeles, I will definitely include The Valley as one of the smartest and best places. I love The Valley. I love everything about it. And I regret all the years of good living I could have had in The Valley if only I had not been such a snob about the West Side.

$1000 Golden Nugget #9
Don't Be Mean To People

You will only end up feeling bad about it.

And that's worse than anything you do to the person.

<u>You</u> are going to keep paying for being mean to that person for years.

In my case, when I was a sophomore in college I was seeing this really nice girl, and I just blew her off one day on her birthday when I was supposed to take her to a reggae concert.

I feel terrible about it even to this day.

She was a really nice person, and she was getting too involved, and I didn't want to go out with her anymore. In itself, all of that is okay – it's just that I did not behave like a gentleman, I just stood her up on her birthday, I went to the Reggae concert with my friends instead of with her, and I'm really really really sorry that I did that.

I did that when I was 19 years old.

That was 24 years ago.

And I still really regret it.

So be nice to people!

ACTION ITEM: This week I want you to use your full name every time you make a reservation at a restaurant or call someone on a work-related call. See if you notice any difference in the way people respond to you and what you want.

14

$2500 GOLDEN NUGGETS

Here's another $22,500 worth of Wharton wisdom.

$2500 Golden Nugget # 1
Lunch With People Often!

Having lunch with people is the best social experience you can have.

Especially if you have more than one lunch with that person. I'm talking about having lunch after lunch after lunch for weeks and weeks and months and months.

When I was in college, I had lunch almost every day of my freshman year with John Favreau, and because of that that, John and I are bonded for the rest of our lives. I'll call him up today and talk to him and it's as easy as it was 6 months into freshman year when we were living across the hall from one another in the Quad. I think it's more about those lunches that we had than about the fact that we became brothers in The Castle or anything else we did together over those 4 years in college.

The fact that we had lunch together all the time was

awesome.

You get to know a person over lunch; it's very casual and very easy to become intimately acquainted with a person when you share all those mealtimes together.

And let me tell you this about that: To me, being intimate and real with people is the real juice in life. You don't get to be truly intimate with all that many people. But simply by having lunch with people over and over and over, you will get that. You will become one of their intimate acquaintances.

After college, I had lunch with one of my contractors -- one of the best guys ever – his name was Scott, and I had lunch with him 2 to 3 times a week for a couples of years while he was building a series of houses for me. When you're having lunch with a person, their guard is down and you really get to know them as a person...

It's a perfect way to get comfortable with them.

So have lunch with people often. It will really pay off. Personally, and financially.

And one more thing about lunches: it's great if you can pay for the other person's lunch all the time. In college we were both on Meal Plans, so nobody was "paying" and it was easy.

But if you're their boss, or you have an expense account, or you have a lot more money than them, treat them to lunch! It's extremely endearing. I know that buying Scott all those hundreds of lunches went a long way towards cementing our great, easy-going relationship. And it felt great too!

$2500 Golden Nugget # 2
Don't Be Jealous

Jealousy will make you do things you that you really don't want to do.

Personally, I have wasted <u>years</u> of my life because I was jealous.

That's all I care really say about that, other than "Don't waste your time on the completely negative emotion of jealousy."

$2500 Golden Nugget #3
Be a Frequent Flyer

Travel as much as you can! Traveling really broadens your perspective on the world and it really enriched my life so much!

By joining the frequent flyer program, I was able to do more traveling, because sometimes you have to do extra traveling in order to be able to take advantage of special mileage offers. Somehow it's more fun when you travel for free on an award ticket!

When I was at Wharton, there was a guy on my freshman floor who was also in Wharton. His name was Enrique Gallo, he was from Nicaragua and he traveled a lot.

One day he came up to me and said "Hey man, are you a Pan Am frequent flyer?"

I said, "No…"

And he goes, "How would you like to go to Europe round

trip for 200 bucks?" I nodded eagerly, and he continued, "I figured out because I am a frequent flyer of Pan Am, they have a special deal going where if you can fly in and out of New York JFK Airport twice, you will earn enough points to get a free round trip ticket to Europe."

The round trip from Philly to New York was a hundred bucks at the time, so Enrique and I took a flight from Philadelphia to New York and back twice. We did it one Friday night and then again the following Friday night. Enrique even got us upgraded to 1st Class because he was such a Frequent Flyer, so we were drinking scotch the whole time and it was one big party for us. It cost me 200 bucks, and that's how I went to Europe my first time – as a Frequent Flyer. It was awesome!

$2500 Golden Nugget # 4
Read Lots of Books

Especially New York Times Bestsellers.

In freshman year, my legal studies professor, Nick Constan, set an indelible example. He told us that he read every single book on the New York Times Non-Fiction Bestseller List.

Now that's an inspiration.

Imagine how much knowledge you're getting from that!

You would think that reading every single New York Time Non-Fiction Bestselling book would be an impossibly huge amount of books for one person to read during the span of a year, but in reality, many books remain on the list for weeks and weeks and weeks, so there's a lot fewer books to read than on the face of it.

Then you would think that a good percentage of those books are on subjects that you're not interested in. But the concept is that if it's good enough to make it onto the list, it's good enough to spend a few hours of your life to see what all the fuss is about. For a book to make it onto the New York Times Bestseller List is a huge accomplishment, and really, is worthy of the fuss and of the attention of a reader.

$2500 Golden Nugget # 5
Don't Be Intimidated by Money

Don't let people who are rich intimidate you.

When I was in college, I had no idea about money; I didn't understand what millionaires really were, even though I was at Wharton, even though I was surrounded by them. I didn't know what that was, and as a result I wasn't intimidated by these people, and I became friends with all these people who were millionaires or who came from millionaire families, or big business families. They were just people to me, just another guy no better than me and no worse.

Unfortunately, after I graduated from Wharton, I lost sight of this all-important little nugget. One day when I was about 27 years old, I was with a friend of mine who was President of Dino De Laurentiis Entertainment, and we were yacht-hopping on the French Riviera during the Cannes Film Festival (during the portion of my career when I was a screenwriter.)

We ended up getting invited onto this enormous yacht. I'm talking about a ship that was 200+ feet long, with a 30-foot speedboat on the deck. That boat itself, the little 30 footer, was probably worth $150 grand. Then there was a Dodge mini-van parked in an on-board garage on the ship, and there was a helicopter on top of it all, ready to go.

So there we were having drinks at the bar with the guy whose boat it was – one of the producers of the Rambo series and of the Terminator II film. As a writer, when you get yourself in front of that kind of person, that's when you're supposed to really turn it on. But unfortunately, I got way too intimidated by all the flash, and I was worthless during my 5 minutes of time with the most powerful guy (at the time) in the film industry. If only I could've just pictured him in his boxer shorts, or somehow forgotten about the money he had. Unfortunately, by that point in my life I had learned what real money was, and I wanted it, and was intimidated by it. So I blew it.

$2500 Golden Nugget #6
Stay Close To Your Alma Mata

You get more value from your education if you stay close to the school. Especially grad school.

After I graduated from Wharton I moved out to California and people were like "Wharton what? What's Wharton?" They had never even heard of Wharton!

On the East Coast, everybody knew what Wharton was, but on the West Coast very very few people knew or cared, and as a result I lost out on a lot of value, especially when looking for jobs, meeting people, networking, and business in general.

A lot of that value of going to Wharton is just to say that you went to Wharton. If people don't know what that means, doesn't get you a lot of value.

This little nugget is especially true when it comes to grad school. If you go to grad school, you have to stay near the grad school. A lot of people in grad school are older, they're married with kids, so they're reluctant to uproot their family after spending two or three or four years in a city. Instead, they stay in the city where the grad school is, where a lot of alumni from the grad school are located and already working and are loyal to the alma matta, so they tap into the alumni network and get as much value from their education investment as they possibly can.

If you're investing years of your time and huge sums of money in an education, you need to be smart about getting all the value out of that investment. Staying close to the school will be a tremendous advantage for you in getting the maximum value from all of your hard work and money.

This little nugget alone is easily worth $10,000 or $20,000 in your very first year after graduation. Think about it: if you don't get a job for a couple of months because you're living in, say, Miami, and nobody cares about UCLA in Miami, and you're a UCLA grad, if you make $1500 a week that's $6 grand a month in lost income. Two months is $12 grand, and three months is $18,000 of lost income. Pretty soon it adds up to some real money! But if you were to stay in Los Angeles, where everyone who is anyone either went to USC or UCLA and everyone has heard of USC and UCLA, then your UCLA education is worth a lot more. You get an obvious advantage over all those shlubbs who went to schools that nobody in Los Angeles has ever heard of, like Wharton.

This advantage is not just in how quickly you get the job, but also in getting the better job that pays the most money. The kind of job that always goes to an insider, someone with a really good network.

So if you want to go to school in the Northeast, it would be really wise if you were to plan on living in the Northeast when you graduate.

There's only 1 exception to this rule. Maybe it's because I didn't go there, and so the grass is always greener on the other side of the fence, but it seems to me that if you go to Harvard you can be exempt from this rule because everyone on the planet is impressed by Harvard.

$2500 Golden Nugget #7
Learn About Wine

Wine is a part of life, and its not going away. It's been here for thousands of years. Wine education and wine savvy is more important now than ever.

So, learn about the different varieties, the different geographic regions that produce wine, what those wines are like, learn what you like in wines, learn what wines generally get paired with what foods, and overall, have a general knowledge of wine. It's extremely helpful, both in social situations and in business.

At the very least you should educate yourself enough about wine so that you don't feel like a total idiot when it comes to buying wine as a gift or ordering a bottle of wine at a restaurant.

The really good news about this is that the way to "educate" yourself about wine is by drinking lots of it – a fun way to learn about something!

Salut!

$2500 Golden Nugget # 8
Be Comfortable in Formal Attire

We had a spring formal and a winter formal every year at The Castle. As a result, wearing a tuxedo became no big deal to me, and that's very good.

There are a lot of very important occasions in life when you're supposed to wear formal attire, and if that's not going to make you uncomfortable, if that's just going to be something that you do with no problem, then you can have a lot more fun at those events, and probably perform better socially at those events as well.

$2500 Golden Nugget # 9
Play Hard & Have Fun

Myles Bass used to always say, "If you're an entrepreneur you're working 168 hours a week." We work all our lives, and most of us work really really really really hard. We deserve to play hard, and to have fun. If you don't, you just become a one-dimensional person, just a drone, and nobody's interested in that.

People are interested in people who know how to have a

good time. People want to be with people who are fun, who know how to have fun, and who enjoy having a good time. If you can't have a good time, then what's it all worth?

ACTION ITEM: I want you to go out and have a really good time one night this week. Do something that you really enjoy. And do it with someone whom you really like spending time with. Go ahead – you deserve it!

15

WHERE IS THE WHARTON SCHOOL?

This chapter is one for everybody.

This chapter will apply to you even if you're not a "business person."

This one is about learning.

It's about knowledge.

It's about becoming a better person.

Not only did my graduation from the Wharton Business School give me the credit of graduating from the very best business school in the world, but I'm also a graduate of Stuyvesant High School, which is obviously the very best high school in New York, and arguably, the very best high school in America, and therefore, quite possibly the best high school in the world. That's right folks, I graduated from the best high school in the world!

I'm laughing right now, because The Best High School In The World is a very dubious distinction. No one will ever ask you where you went to high school as part of a job interview.

I wasn't trying to impress you with this academic credential, but I was trying to impress something upon you. And that is, after graduating from the best business school and one of the top universities in America, and the best high school in the world, I think I know a thing or two about learning, how to learn, where to learn, why to learn, etc. And that's what this little discourse is all about... learning.

So the main question for me is where do you learn?

Do you learn on your mamma's knee?

Do you learn in the schoolyard?

Do you learn on the mean streets?

Or do you learn in the classroom?

After all, I've attended many of the very finest classrooms in America, if not the world. I've learned a lot of stuff. I really have. In high school I had 95 GPA, and in college I had a 4.0 GPA in my major. I've been a top student for many many many years of my career as a student, and I graduated from some of the best schools in the country. So where did I learn?

I'll tell you something folks: for the most part, learning does not occur in the classroom.

In fact, in order to get in to Stuyvesant high school, I had a tutor, because I was such a lousy student. My parents got me a tutor so that I could pass the entrance exam and get into Stuyvesant high school. So a lot of learning I did, was right at my kitchen table with the tutor sitting there picking his nose and scratching it off on the under side of his chair. Honestly, that's exactly what happened. But that guy taught me how to do multiplication, division, fractions, English, vocabulary and sentence structure... blah blah blah. He taught me everything that I needed to know to pass that exam and get into Stuyvesant High School. And if it weren't for that guy, I would not have gotten in. So all that learning I needed did not occur in a classroom, it occurred in my home.

Then I wanted to go to the Wharton Business School. I had to get those SAT scores, right? I mean, I scored 1390 on my SATs, when the maximum you could get was 1600. Not a bad score, top 97th percentile.

So how did I do that? Was it because of what I learned in The Best High School In The World, in the classrooms there?

No.

Once again, the learning took place outside of the classrooms. They don't teach you how to take the SAT's in high school. So, Saturday mornings, there I was at Stanley Kaplan's upon 53rd street learning how to become an expert at the SATs. That's right, I went to PSAT training at Kaplan's, then I went to SAT training at Kaplan's, and I actually had Stanley Kaplan's son, Paul Kaplan, as my teacher, and he used to say, "If I'm talking too fast, then you have to think faster." That guy was a really smart guy, and a great teacher who taught us everything we needed to know to become masters of the SAT.

So did the learning take place in the classroom? No. It happened in the extra classroom, during my extracurricular activities after school. On Saturday mornings! I remember going uptown on the subway together with my best friend Jackie Ewenstein on Saturday mornings at 9 o'clock in order to get to Kaplan's for our SAT training. She got "Double 760's" on her SATs and went on to graduate from Harvard, Phi Beta

Kappa. All my friends went to Harvard!

Then I went to college, the Wharton Business School.

Where did the learning take place there?

I told you in a previous chapter that one of the biggest lessons I learned at Wharton did not take place in the classroom. It took place in the home of my entrepreneurial management professor, Myles Bass, the greatest professor of all time. And he taught me that everything matters. Everything, everything.

So again, the learning did not take place in the classroom, not even at Wharton.

And having said that, let me say this about that -- and that would be this: The single most important thing that I ever learned is something that I did learn in class. It was from my professor whose name was Digby Baltzell. He actually invented the term WASP -- White Anglo-Saxon Protestant. He invented that. And in the final chapter of this book, which is entitled: How To Know If You've Lived A Successful Life, I'll reveal that single most important thing that I ever learned anywhere from anyone. Thank you.

But to continue with this chapter...

I think the clearest way to explain it is this: after you graduate from college and there is no more classroom, does the learning stop? No!

The learning need not ever stop.

The learning takes place whenever you open a book, wherever that will be, in high school, college, after college, it's all the same.

You don't learn in the class.

You learn in the context of the class.

Because you're a student of XYZ subject, whatever subject you are studying, you will learn about that subject because the classroom is not the class. The classroom is just a context of the class.

All of these things that I learned from high school, college, and after college, were learned outside the class.

I learned them in the palm of my hand, holding that book

Then, especially after college, I learned in the field. I learned from experience. I learned how to build a whole damn house! Nobody's going to teach you that in college. Nobody's going to teach you that in contractor school. Nobody teaches you that anywhere! You have to learn that from experience. You have to learn by doing.

Most of the learning that you're going to do is going to be for some class that you're taking, and yes it is absolutely essential to show up, attendance absolutely matters, not because you're going to be learning the majority of your stuff that you're going to learn by being in that class -- the majority of learning that you're going to do is going to take place outside of the classroom. Its going to be in your bedroom, in your living room, on a train, waiting for the bus, at the beach, in an airplane, wherever you may be, wherever you may be reading, wherever you may be practicing, wherever you may be experimenting, that's where the learning takes place.

So why even bother going to Wharton? Right? Why bother going to Stuyvesant high school?

Well, it's not the place.

It is not the place.

There are 2 reasons why you should go to Wharton.

There are 2 reasons why you should go to Stuyvesant High School, or the best high school or university you can get into.

Number 1 is The People.

College is all about socializing, meeting people, making friends, creating a network for yourself of people who understand you, who you understand, who you respect, and who are going places.

And Number 2, learning is a state of mind. More than anything else, its about having an image of yourself as a Wharton student, as a Stuyvesant High School student, as a Harvard Student and then being that student because that is the picture that you've created for yourself, in your own mind.

ACTION ITEM: Go to Wikipedia or any type of encyclopedia and teach yourself something new. Learn. Transform yourself through the magic of reading and the perspective of being a student.

16

DIAMONDS

In this chapter I've got diamonds for you.

I had so much fun with the Golden Nuggets that I decided to put together two more collections of gems: "Diamonds" and "Superstars" for the next chapters.

Diamonds is a collection of shorter subjects that were too short to have their own chapter, but too long to make them just nuggets.

Diamond #1

Use Top Technology

Always use the best technology you can get your hands on. This applies to telephones, answering systems, email, computers, vehicles... whenever your life intersects with technology, get the best you can possibly afford.

We live in a technological era.

Everything is moving at the speed of light.

You cannot afford to waste your time doing things the old fashioned way. You cannot afford to do it manually. You have to do it, whatever it is, with the best technology available to you.

When I was in high school, I had to literally go out and buy myself an IBM Selectric typewriter. That was an electric typewriter, which was the best you could have in that day. I used it in junior and senior of high school, and I even used it in my freshman year of college (because we weren't computerized then.)

In 1984, my sophomore year of college, the University of Pennsylvania made a university-wide deal with Apple Computer, and students got to have a discounted price on the brand new Apple Macintosh. I think it cost me $1900, and I got a 128K Macintosh computer, the square one. It used to make all sorts of humming noises, "Voooooooo-doohhh-djjshhhhhhhhhhh-dhhhhsuhhsh." It was a lot of fun!

I used the hell out of that computer.

I believed at that time, and I still do, that you need to have documents that were flawless. If they looked good, that was half the battle. If you handed in documents that had cross outs or typos or bad printing, you were starting off with one foot in the ditch. But if your document looked perfect, it was that much harder for the teacher to make little notes on it, usually deducting points off your essay or your test or whatever you were doing. So I would always print my stuff out on laser printers – I would go to Kinko's and pay to have it printed out on laser printers, so that it would look perfect.

At the time, I was also very much into my own voicemail and telephone system. Now remember, in those days, we were still using tapes for voicemail messages, so everyone had their own answering machine in their home. When I had a roommate, we each had our own phone line, and we each had our own voicemail message, and we each had our own answering machine.

And speaking of answering machines...

You have to have a great outgoing voicemail message. Especially if you are a businessperson, and especially if you are a man, you want a voicemail message that is clear, that states your whole entire name and that you sound good in. That your voice sounds good in. You have to sound like a person that you would want to be contacting. You don't want to sound weird, you don't want to sound effeminate, you want to sound like a <u>man</u> leaving a voicemail message.

I also am very particular about people saying their whole name. I think everyone should say their whole name on their voicemail message. Unless you're just a kid, unless you don't care about anyone who may want to hire you, or pay you, or give you money for any reason. If you don't care about money, then you could just say, "Hi my name is Joe leave a message." Or you could say "Hello? ... Hello? ... Hello? Oh, I'm not here right now, that was just a trick!" You could play that trick, that stupid voicemail trick about making people think you're actually answering the phone. It kills me when people do that.

Anyway, you need a great outgoing voicemail message, and then, in this age of technology, you need to know how to leave a good message. You need to make sure that you say your full name and leave your number twice, once at the beginning and once at the end of the message, and you have to be able to speak clearly so that people can understand what the hell you are saying in your message.

Nothing bothers me more, and nothing makes me and my

wife make fun of people more than when they leave me a voicemail message on my answering machine or on my voicemail system and I cannot understand what the hell they are saying. Man! We always play them for each other, and laugh at the people.

Technology -- get the best you can, and use it to leverage your power and effectiveness for all it's worth.

Diamond #2

Be Friends With Your Neighbors

This is a very important concept.

We live in the world. No man is an island.

Okay, you live in the city, and it's the big bad city.

Well, shouldn't that be extra reason why you should be able to know your neighbors? To try and personalize the big bad city that we live in?

In college, knowing my neighbors was some of the most important things that happened to me. I became friends with some of the most cool and important people in my life, people whom I got to know <u>because</u> they were my neighbors. Either they were my neighbors in my dorm, like Enrique Gallo, or John Favreau, or they were my neighbors in the fraternity (like every one of my fraternity brothers I knew,) or they were my neighbors in my little apartment building, or on my block.

I knew the people.

And it was very helpful to become friends with them that way, just because we were neighbors.

Moving forward in the future, after college, knowing my

neighbors has also been a great boon to my life.

It helps if your dog escapes. Your neighbor could find the dog, and return it to you.

It helps to hang out and socialize with your neighbors. To have low-key cocktails with them and not have to worry about drinking and driving because everyone just walks home.

It helps because people will look out for you, people will keep an eye on you.

And then people may end up doing business with you. You may find, low and behold, that you have more in common with your neighbors than you would think. Which is not surprising because out of all the places in the world, you both decide to live in a certain little part of town on a certain street, the odds are that you have other vibratory frequencies in common.

So get to know your neighbors. Be friends with them, be nice to them, be helpful to them. Be open to possibilities with them. It's a moveable feast.

Diamond #3
Know & Respect Your Body Clock

This one is so important, especially to a person like me, who is not a morning person.

It took me until about junior year of high school, to understand this issue. Luckily for me, I was able to plan my schedule, even in high school, so that I didn't have to appear in school, until 10:15 a.m. Man, that was awesome!

Then, when I went to college, during my first semester of freshman year, I had no choice I had to take a calculus class at

930 a.m. on Tuesdays and Thursdays. The way they had it set up was that you had a hour lecture once a week with 300 or so students in the lecture hall, then you had two small "recitation" classes, where you would go and it would be only like 30 or 40 kids with a grad student who would answer some of your more advanced or more individualized questions than you could get to in a lecture with three or four hundred people. So, I had that Tuesday, Thursday recitation class at 930, and man I could not get there! It was way across campus and 930 was way to early because I'm not a morning person, and also, my fraternity was having parties on Wednesday nights, (just about every other Wednesday night there was a party at my fraternity house, so I had to go to that of course.)

Got a D in calculus that first semester. Bummer!

However, that next semester I got out of that class and had an afternoon recitation. Somehow I managed to get a ten-thirty recitation, and I was able to get that last B in calculus. That's right, I worked my ass off for that. So, know and respect your body clock.

If you're not a morning person, don't sign up for classes first thing in the morning. Don't schedule yourself for meetings first thing in the morning.

Especially if you're an entrepreneur.

That goes into the body clock of the city in which you live. If the city in which you live has a standard rush hour that goes from, lets say, 7:30 to 9:30, then don't make appointments for yourself across town at 9 or 9:30 or 8 o'clock in the morning if you're an entrepreneur.

If you're an entrepreneur you should not be driving in rush

hour traffic. That is my firm and solid and honest belief.

I try never to drive in rush hour traffic.

I try always to schedule my driving so that it takes place in non-peak rush-hour traffic. Mid-day. 10 o'clock in the morning until 2:30, and then after 7:30 p.m. That's when I want to be driving. Until 7 o'clock in the morning. Other times, I don't want to drive.

Diamond #4
Quality

Quality is a basic assumption.

If you do not have an outstanding product, just forget it.

Nobody wants it.

Nobody wants garbage.

Nobody wants crap.

The only thing people want is something that is great.

So if you don't have something great, don't even bother.

We try to get away with whatever we can get away with, but at the bottom line, in the long run, in the end, its got to be great or else don't even bother.

If it's not great, just go home, go to sleep and start again the next day, because it ain't gonna work.

ACTION ITEM: Hang out with one of your neighbors and get to know them better. Invite them over for a cocktail after work, or take your dogs for a walk around the neighborhood together, or just go over to their house and tell that appreciate their garden you'd like to hang out and admire their flowers and visit together for a little while. Have fun and enjoy the people in your world.

17

SUPERSTARS

These concepts will help you become a Superstar.

Superstar Rule #1 : Have A Dream

Today (the day that I am writing this) is Martin Luther King Day in the United States, and so it is fitting that we get right into this chapter with an item that is really inspired by Martin Luther King. It's something that I learned the importance of while I was at Wharton, and subsequent to graduating, it's become more and more important. It is the idea that you must have a dream.

If you don't have a dream the days are going to be too cold and dark, but if you do have a dream, if you dare to have a dream, you will always be giving yourself hope, you will always be giving yourself something to work for, something that is bigger than just your everyday life.

So in this chapter of little Superstar ideas and concepts, I want to begin with a tribute to Martin Luther King and encourage everyone who is reading this to dare and have a dream. For yourself, for your children, for your co-workers, employees, clients -- everyone is counting on you to dream.

Superstar Rule #2: Have Fun

If you're not having fun, you're doing it wrong.

Life cannot only be about work.

Life has to have fun in it, or else, you won't want to live anymore.

When I was in high school I always had fun. I had fun riding my bike around New York City, I had fun hanging out with my friends, I had fun lifting weights with my buddies on the wrestling team, I had fun being a championship wrestler, I had fun performing...

All of that was part of what it took to get into the Wharton Business School.

Then, when I was at Wharton, some of the greatest things that I did were pure "fun events." Pledging my fraternity, having lunches with my friends, taking classes that interested me, being very active in the party and social scene, dating, travel, etc.

All of that fun was instrumental to my being able to complete the four years of blood, sweat, tears, and big bucks that were required for me to graduate Wharton. If I hadn't been having fun, I never would have made it.

Subsequent to graduating, fun has played an essential element in my success, as a businessman, as an entrepreneur.

Over the several years of the real estate boom I've bought and sold a number houses, and part of my marketing strategy for selling the houses was always to have lots of parties. I figured that the more people who knew about the house, saw the house, loved the house, ultimately the better it would be when it came time for me to sell.

And it worked out. I've sold houses at top dollar all the way through, even at the end when the real estate boom had already ended, or was already in the decline, I was still getting excellent money for my houses. A lot of that was due to the fun that I had.

And also it was due to how we designed the houses to be fun houses to live in, and fun houses to party in, and fun houses to work in. Fun was an element in all of that.

I cannot recommend highly enough that you devote significant mental resources, time, and attention, to having fun. You wont be sorry.

Superstar Rule #3 : Have A Really Cool Home

I've always had really cool homes.

Always!

Even in high school, when I didn't like my parents house, and I didn't like the clutter, at least I had my own room, and I painted it, and de-cluttered it, and added extra walls in it, and made it my own, and it was cool.

I remember when I painted one of my walls Citibank Blue. We had a Citibank right across the street from where I was growing up, and that was the color that I picked. I just loved it.

I remember painting it, and just standing there, marveling at how great the room looked with that blue wall! It was awesome.

It was in that room with the blue wall that I came up with the dream -- and made it happen -- of getting into the Wharton

Business School and attending the best business school in the world.

I think that my cool environment helped me to do that.

Once I got into Wharton I always had cool homes.

I lived in The Quad freshman year, in a newly renovated room, overlooking ivy-decked courtyards, and it was awesome.

Sophomore year I lived in The Castle. I lived in a castle. It doesn't get much cooler than that.

That place had wainscoting on the walls, a huge fireplace in the Great Hall with a giant elk head over the fireplace...

Even my room, which I shared with my roommate Evan -- I got us this special combination key pad lock, so that our possessions would be secure, and we wouldn't have to worry about keys, all we had to do was enter the combination on the lock and enter into our super cool Fortress, which is what we called it.

Then junior year, gosh, I had an amazing apartment! One of my fraternity brothers, Todd Simon, sublet me his unbelievable duplex 1-bedroom about a block and a half away from campus. And not only was my apartment super cool, but the neighbors and friends that I met were super cool. One of them became a business partner of mine, and another one became a future roommate of mine: in senior year, David Rothschild, had been my upstairs neighbor in the little apartment building on Pine Street, then the following year I moved in with him in his ultra super cool luxury apartment downtown. I rented a bedroom from him, it was a total luxury building, and a really great living environment.

After college, I've always tried to have super cool places to live.

You spend so much time at home. It shapes and influences all the vibrations of your life.

You owe it to yourself and your friends and all the people you care about to create a living environment for yourself which inspires you, which makes you feel special, which makes you feel good about yourself, which allows you to live a peaceful, harmonious, and happy life.

If you're suffering from too much noise, or a view of a brick wall, or cramped quarters, or squalid conditions, there is no way that you're going to be able to really elevate yourself out of that without extra super extraordinary endeavors on your part. Take a couple of extra weeks when you're searching for your home to find one that's really cool, because having a cool home is one of the key things that I learned at the Wharton Business School.

Superstar Rule #4: Read & Write Well

In this day and age of interconnected communications it's more important than ever to be a great reader and writer.

You are always communicating with e-mails, with memos, with Facebook posts and Twitter tweets... Twitter tweets are little poems in the hands of the right author! And powerful sales tools that have pried real dollars out of MY hands.

As far as reading well, there is nothing you can't learn if you're a good reader. There is nothing you can't teach yourself if you're a good reader. Especially valuable is the skill of reading for entertainment purposes. I mean, yeah, there's television and movies but nothing replaces an afternoon by the fire or on the beach with a good book. Nothing replaces that.

Likewise, nothing is more invaluable than the right book at the right time in the hands of the right person. It's how you can teach yourself anything!

Most of the learning that I did in college was just from reading. And a lot of the learning I've done since college has been from reading.

I remember there were some hard times in my life, in my mid 30s, and that's when Frank McCourt's book, "Angela's Ashes," came out. He subsequently won the Pulitzer prize for that book.

Frank was my creative writing teacher at Stuyvesant High School, and for many cold nights when I was living on my boat in Marina del Rey, the only solace that I had was when I would pull out Frank McCourt's book and I would read any given chapter from "Angela's Ashes." It was so inspirational and so beautiful! It was just so beautiful to read that gorgeous prose. I'll never forget those times, and I encourage everyone to be an avid reader, to enjoy reading, both for your own entertainment and for your personal betterment.

Superstar Rule #5: The Back of The Envelope Rule

"Never do any deal you cannot explain on the back of an envelope." – Myles Bass

If you want to be a superstar, you've got to know how to keep things SIMPLE.

18

THE MOST IMPORTANT THING
I EVER LEARNED

Chapter 18 is a very special, powerful, unbelievable chapter for me because this is the final chapter of what I've got to say about what I learned at the best business school in the world. And it's coming at a very auspicious time. I'm writing this on the last day of the first retrograde mercury in 2009, and I'm going all the way back, pulling out everything I've got, to give it to you.

That's right folks, I started this project several months ago, capturing all the best stuff I learned, all the most important stuff, all the most meaningful stuff, and now I can look back at the chapters that I've written, and see that the information is really really comprehensive and detailed – everything I learned from my four years of blood, sweat, tears and having paid the big bucks to attend an Ivy league university and get the best business school education that you can get in the world.

And now it all comes down to this chapter.

This chapter that I've been talking about and hyping for a

long time, contains the most important piece of information that I have ever learned in my entire life. That's right folks.

I learned it from one of the most illustrious professors in the whole university. His name was E. Digby Baltzell. He taught it to me in the very last class that he ever taught at the University of Pennsylvania. He retired right after I got done taking his class. And, man, I learned a lot of important stuff from that guy.

One thing he taught me was the most important thing ever, but I did learn something else that I think was really key, so I'm going to give you an extra bonus here. Not just the most important thing that I learned, but an extra bonus that I learned from E. Digby Baltzell. And I learned both of these things in his class.

As I talked about in a previous chapter, how learning doesn't necessarily take place in the classroom, well, here's an extra lesson for you, okay? Now, I was a graduating senior when I took Digby's class, Social Stratification in America. And one of the golden rules of his class was, if you were a graduating senior and you took his class, you were guaranteed a "Gentleman's C" as long as you took all of the exams. But more importantly than that, he said "If you're a graduating senior in my class and you get an A in any one of the midterms, then you don't have to come to class anymore, and you don't have to take any more tests." If you can demonstrate mastery of the material, and get an A, in any midterm exam, that was it, you got an A for the class.

So, there I am, Mr. Graduating Senior, Hotshot Wharton Man, taking Digby's class. Of course I get an A on the first midterm! So, now I'm guaranteed an A for the class, I don't have to take any more tests, and I don't even have to show up for any more lectures.

Do you think that I continue to attend the class?

There were plenty of friends of mine who were graduating seniors. They got that A, and they were gone. What the hell did they need to go to that class for?

But you see, I appreciated the value of what I was getting.

Here I have a living legend teaching my class, you better believe my ass was in the seat for every single lecture that man gave us.

It didn't matter how nice it was outside, it didn't matter that it was Spring and the birds were chirping and the grass was green out on college lawn. No way. I was in College Hall, listening to every word that Digby Baltzell had to say, because that was the intense kind of student that I was. That's the way I treated my four-year college education with respect. That's the amount of respect I had for being a Wharton Business School student.

And I believe it paid off, because if I hadn't been attending all those lectures that I was already exempted from, I never would have heard the most important thing that I ever learned in any class, or any educational institution that I ever attended. And so, lesson number one from Mr. Digby Baltzell was "Attend the classes!"

Even when the teacher says you don't have to, attend the classes. Because, on the last day of the last class that Digby Baltzell ever taught, I was there instead of out getting a sun tan in the spring sunlight with the rest of the slackers. And, because

I was sitting in my seat, I learned the most important thing that I have ever learned from anyone.

He got real somber and serious when he said it. And this is a man who was in his 70's at the time, and he looked it. He was old -- wearing a bowtie -- one of those old time Ivy League professors. A wise and brilliant man. He actually coined the term WASP – white Anglo-Saxon protestant -- he created POP culture when he coined the term WASP, a key concept in our American society.

Digby Baltzell said this: "If, by the time you die, you have one true friend, then you have lived a successful life."

What do you think about that?

What do you think about the fact that it all comes down to one friend?

Man, it makes me really value the people that I have in my life.

It makes me not take for granted, the friends that I have, and that I've kept for all of these years. It makes me grateful to have those people in my life.

But more than that, it makes me extremely grateful to have found my wife, my mate, my soul mate, Alison, because I know that she's so much more than a friend, but for sure she is a true friend.

And it makes me really appreciate the institution of marriage and the idea that there is someone out there for everyone.

I think what Digby was really talking about, was this institution of marriage, even though he didn't say it. Even though he didn't enumerate it in any way. I understood when I was sitting there, that he was talking about his wife.

I understood that when he said if you have one true friend by the time you die, that you have lived a successful life, that he was thinking about his wife, and how lucky he was to have her. Because if you can have one true friend, that makes everything worthwhile.

It makes all the difference in the entire world.

Think about the difference between these two scenarios: 1) You're sitting at an outdoor cafe in Rome, you have a great table with a perfect cappuccino on a gorgeous spring day, birds are chirping, the sunlight is glinting off the water cascading down the sculpted face of a centuries-old public fountain, and you're all alone. 2) You're sitting at the same great table at the same phenomenal outdoor cafe, its a beautiful day with the sun shining off the water in the beautiful marble fountain, and you're sharing it with your one true friend in life – your soul-mate.

Which of those scenarios would be immeasurably better than the other one?

My father said something to me a number of times, but I didn't really understand it when he said it.

He said, "I'm your father -- who the hell else do you think gives shit about you?"

I didn't understand it when he was alive, but now that he's gone and I've gained some perspective, I think I understand what he was really trying to say: Nobody really cares about anyone else.

I've got all of these friends -- and I honestly do have a blessing of friends, that's how many friends I have; I am blessed -- but when it all comes down to it, the only one that REALLY REALLY cares about me is my one true friend, which is my wife.

If I were to die tomorrow, all my friends would be sad – maybe even for more than a couple of days! But pretty soon they would just get back to their normal everyday lives, and life would just go on as normal for them. Maybe they would miss me from time to time, or talk about me, remember me, perhaps even tell stories about me – but for the most part, nothing would change for them. And the same goes for me. If any of my friends were to disappear, my life would pretty much continue unchanged.

But with my wife it's completely different. Having her in my life makes all the difference in the world. It makes every single dinner that I share with her a special occasion. It makes every special trip that I take with her, traveling the world, something that we shared. Everything that I do with her is a special moment that I share with somebody who truly cares about me. Someone who truly cares about our time together.

It makes all the difference in the world.

POSTSCRIPT

My gratitude to professor E. Digby Baltzell for sharing so many years of wisdom with me and with all the thousands of students at the university to which he dedicated his life.

If you would like more training in the art and science of being an entrepreneur, please check out www.ClintArthur.com for the full suite of available materials, including new Video Trainings on What They Teach You At The Wharton Business School featuring me and other Wharton Entrepreneurs I've had the pleasure to know.

I hope that you will write to me with any comments or testimonials, or just to share your experience of how this has impacted your life. I really look forward to that.

Email those comments: Clint@ClintArthur.com

THANK YOU!

A few words about…

The Last Year Of Your Life

I've got a question for you: Do you think it's possible for a person like you to transform your life in just one year's time so that you're getting twice as much of all The Good Stuff?

By The Good Stuff, I mean that your relationships with people you really care about, like family, friends, co-workers, clients – even your relationship with your self – do you think it's possible to have relationships which are twice as deep, twice as meaningful, twice as real?

What about your physical fitness, vitality, and health? Could you be twice as healthy as you've ever been as an adult?

What about your level of spiritual fulfillment – could that double? Could you be living with twice as much spiritual fulfillment in your life?

How about your income – do you think it's possible for you to double your income in just one year's time, and accomplish all the rest?

A lot of people know my story… I was a taxi driver, surviving on less than $500 a week, living underwater! Literally! I was on a small boat, and it was so cold at night in the winter-time that I would sleep with all my heaviest clothes on, wrapped up in a heavy down comforter, and it was so cold that I could see my breath coming out of my mouth – that's how freezing it was.

I was beginning to become terrified that I would never be able to escape the rut that had become my life over that 5-year period of time, so I started doing massive amounts of self-help work. I did everything: The Artist's Way, Rich Dad Poor Dad, Carlton Sheets, Deepak Chopra, Tony Robbins, The Four Agreements, I did men's power ceremonies, and I walked on fire!

Then one day a man said something to me that would change my life. He said, "You don't know it yet, but you're already dead!"

I said to myself, What the hell does that mean? Do I have a date with destiny, or something? What does he mean I'm already dead? You're already dead... You're already dead!

I couldn't get that out of my mind.

Then it came to be New Year's Day and I sat down to write out my list of goals for the year, as I do on every New Year's Day, and that year I had a divine inspiration. I asked myself a question: What would you want to do this year if this was going to be the last year of your life?

That question inspired me and my whole circle of people in my life.

That year I lost forty pounds and went from a size forty waist to a thirty-six.

I opened a factory to produce the product I'd been buying from a manufacturer in another state. As a result, I was able to triple my company's profits and simultaneously reduce costs for my clients by 21 percent—this had been an unachieved dream of mine for almost five years!

I even sat down and wrote a book about the lessons I learned at the Wharton Business School, which was something I had been putting off for almost ten years.

Most importantly, with the help of my wife I was able to turn around my marriage—which had been experiencing some serious rough going at the 7-year mark—to the point where today, as I write this, we've been together 10 years, my wife and I both feel that our life together is better than ever and our future together looks more promising than ever.

Other people who have done The Last Year Of Your Life Program have also gotten amazing results. One man had been playing guitar and singing his whole life, but he had never recorded anything until The Last Year of Your Life Program, when he recorded an entire album of original music.

Another member, at the age of sixty-three (!), barely had two nickels to rub together when they started, but that year they wrote a business plan, found an investor, and opened a cupcake store in a major regional mall in Southern California. This summer their kids were working in the cupcake store! (How cool is that?!)

And last summer, a woman fulfilled her dream of praying at her religion's holiest sites when she flew to the Middle East and did just that for two weeks.

Along the way to achieving these tremendous milestones, members of the program practiced daily meditation and exercise; they expressed gratitude; they became healthier, happier, expanded their concept of what was possible, and treated their loved ones — and people they met in the street — with more respect and admiration than ever before.

Now how do you put a price on achieving a closer relationship with your God or higher power, with your spouse or your kids, achieving artistic or business aspirations? You can't – those are priceless results!

That's the difference between living The Last Year Of Your Life and having a bucket list. With a bucket list, you jump out of an airplane, you drive an Indy race car, and you fulfill a whole bunch of purely personal self-indulgent fantasy experiences so you don't feel like you missed out on anything. But with The Last Year Of Your Life you fulfill your hearts deepest longings and desires, you do things that are going to live beyond your lifetime, that are going to create a legacy.

Living The Last Year Of Your Life is one of the most exhilarating and rewarding experiences I've ever known, and I have designed this workbook to deliver the same results for you.

You can start on January first, or at any moment in time, and begin a personal journey in which you experience the Last Year of Your Life. Do it alone; do it with a friend, coworker, colleague, or with family members. Men or women, young or old, the more the better—there's power in numbers!

All that matters is that you begin in earnest and live each day moving forward as if it is precious, and as if it were one of your last. Once you do this, your life will never be the same.

If you want to be part of an organized twelve-month online or live program, go to www.TheLastYearofYourLife.com and join the community of people all around the world who are living with a passion you can only get when you live as if you only have fifty-two weeks left on this earth.

The Last Year Of Your Life is dedicated to your success, fulfillment, and the greatness of your own life, and I salute you for having the courage to really go for it!

Sincerely,

CLINT ARTHUR

THE INCOME DOUBLER

Are You Sick And Tired Of Not Being A Rising Star or a Superstar in Your Business?

The good news is that you have just discovered a field-tested, simple system that makes it easy for ANY ENTREPRENEUR to get so hot at what they are doing, they actually double their income in 180 days or less -- and it comes with a Double Your Money Back Guarantee...

Dear Fellow Entrepreneur,

Three years ago I was probably just like you, moving forward with my business, but not able to truly break through. My income was enough to get by, but not exciting. My customer list was steady, but not growing. My business life -- and the rest of my life -- was okay, but stagnant. And that actually concerned me -- because you know, you're either growing or you're dying -- right?

Because it was the recession, I didn't beat myself up too bad about it, but I started doing lots of self-help work to try and turn things around.

Luckily, I happened to take an amazing seminar called *Train Your Brain For Success* with Robert Irwin, PhD., and at that seminar he taught us that you can re-program your subconscious mind to "trick yourself" into believing whatever you want to believe -- and that if you believed you deserved something, your subconscious mind would make it a reality for you. Kinda like *The Secret*.

So I decided that I was going to make myself believe I deserved to be earning twice as much as I was earning. And whaddaya know -- it actually worked! Not because I was chanting "OM" in my dark room all day, but because the process of retraining my brain got me off my assets and into action.

It was amazing! To be able to set a huge goal like that and make it happen -- what a rush! What a feeling of accomplishment! What a confidence builder! What fun!

As soon as I achieved my goal of doubling my income, I was so excited that I put together a group of friends and business associates and taught them exactly what I did, and lead them through the experience on weekly conference calls. 6 out of 10 finished the 180-day program, and every one that finished either doubled their income, came really close to it, or exceeded that goal! It was amazing, and a lot of fun...

The Science of The Income Doubler: 95% of your brain is controlled by your subconscious mind. This is the section of your brain that automates body processes such as breathing and your heartbeat, and actions such as driving a car, which you can do "absent-mindedly" -- your subconscious runs you through these processes automatically.

Because of these automatic "tape loops" in your subconscious mind, 85% of all your thoughts today are the same as yesterday's. This is why people's lives remain basically the same -- the vast majority of their thoughts are the same, day after day, year after year.

The final piece of the puzzle is that whatever your subconscious mind believes to be true, becomes your reality. If your subconscious mind believes that you deserve income of $20,000 a year, that's what you'll earn. If it believes you deserve the life of a billionaire, then you get to be Donald Trump or Warren Buffett.

The Income Doubler is a system to guide you in the process of reprogramming your subconscious mind to believe you are worth twice as much as you currently earn, and as soon as you believe that, you will double your income.

The process is very simple: You write out a specific goal for your income a number of times every day for 180 days. As you go along, you will feel your self-confidence, motivation, and initiative building -- and with that, you will see your income building.

My Action Guide is a book you will use to keep you on track. It has room for you to do your daily writing, and little motivation quotes and stories from my business and other exploits to keep entertained along the way. That's all you need. It takes about 15 minutes a day -- that's it! Yes, it's that easy.

All you have to do is a little writing and talking to yourself every day for 6 months, believe in the process, and let the power of The Income Doubler system do it's work.

So you have nothing to risk, and everything to gain!

Imagine how great your life would be if you had twice as much money every month! Would you finally take a real vacation? Get a new car? Do something that's a once-in-a-lifetime experience with your spouse?

This will be the smartest investment you've ever made....

Sincerely,

CLINT ARTHUR

Dear Fellow Author, Expert, Speaker, or Entrepreneur:

18 months ago I was an author/expert/entrepreneur with no TV news interviews to show anyone — I mean, ZERO. Now I have 33 interviews and appearances on local TV stations across the USA, including many FOX, ABC, NBC, and CBS Network affiliate stations in top 10 Nielsen Markets like Chicago, Boston, Houston, and San Francisco...

Over the course of my experiences, I have learned that you do not have to be a celebrity or a PR Professional to get booked onto these local TV shows — in fact it's actually easier and better for you to book yourself onto these programs — and not only is it easier and better, but it's completely FREE!

With my New TV Power system you get a complete program to take you from a total Zero to a TV News Hero, including all the names and phone numbers of Producers at all the Network Affiliate TV stations in the Top 100 markets in the United States, as well as their email addresses, their physical addresses, and I will train you in just 5 hours so that you know everything YOU NEED TO KNOW in order to be an IRRESISTIBLE Guest that TV Producers will book over and over and over.

- The 2 types of segments that will get you booked on TV News and talk shows...(I break it all down so it's as simple as A or B.)

- ***The 5 MUST-HAVE elements to make your pitch like CATNIP to TV Producers...(So that they become like purring kittens in your hands.)***

- How to talk to Producers to make them believe you are a credible guest and not a rank amateur...(so that you're so convincing that they could actually book you off a voice-mail message — I've done it! — and re-book you any time you want.)

- ***The 2 types of phone calls you will make to get yourself booked... (so you know what kind of call to make every single time you pick up the phone to call a producer.)***

- How to effectively use my vast database of personal contacts...(It's a huge amount of information, but I make it really easy for you to harvest all it's power.)

- ***How to dress in order to get the most out of your TV appearances...(you don't need good looks or money to come off like a pro on TV!)***

- How to act ON SET and IN STUDIO to maximize every opportunity available to you during a TV appearance... (these in-studio guest appearances are like GOLD, and I want you to be able to mine each and every vein for all they're worth.)

- ***How to get clips of your segments, regardless of when or where they occur...(You are doing this to get the clips, and I'll tell you the best and cheapest way to get them, and the formats you need them to be in so you can use them on your website.)***

- How to turn 1 booking into 5, 6, 7 or more bookings on the same station... (If you follow my instructions you'll get on TV so much it will make your head spin.)

- ***How to use your New TV Power to save $1000's on your TAXES! (Using this 1 strategy will put your investment in the New TV Power system into profits several times over. And it's so obvious and easy to do you'll actually say, "Duhhhh!")***

- Bonus Magical Powers you can only get by appearing on television... (You ever wonder why celebrities seem to get their way and get away with stuff all the time? It's because you get actual Magical Powers by appearing on TV all the time. I'll tell you what they are, and how to use them to advance your personal, professional, and spiritual goals.)

■ *10 ways to leverage local publicity for Personal, Professional, and Spiritual advancement... (I keep talking about Personal and Spiritual stuff, and I'm not kidding. I will show you and explain to you exactly why becoming a Micro-Superstar is the best thing you could ever do for your personal development, and the most important thing you will ever do for your spiritual mission on this earth.* **But don't worry, if you just want to use your New TV Power to make more money, that's fine too.)**

Dylan on NBC – His Very First TV Appearance

Later that Morning… Dylan on ABC

New TV Power Student Books Himself on FOX CT

YOU GET 4 DVD's — A COMPLETE VIDEO TRAINING PROGRAM takes you all the way from concept creation, to pitching, to studio tips, to embedding the clips on your website.. You will watch me making actual calls to real live producers all across the country... complete with critiques and instructions inserted into the action... and resulting in 2 actual TV bookings onto local Network Affiliates.

PLUS – videos of the actual segments I did on those stations you watched me call into to get booked, so you can see how the segments get translated from the PITCH to the PERFORMANCE!

PLUS 3 AUDIO CD's packed with hours more of unique and exclusive training in the real techniques and methods my students and I use every day to book ourselves on TV shows across the country. This is not theory, this is not ideology — this is what is actually working right NOW for Regular People like you and me!

AND YOU ALSO GET...

9 DIFFERENT SEGMENT PROPOSALS WRITTEN BY ME AND MY STUDENTS THAT ARE ACTUALLY BEING USED IN "THE FIELD" AND GETTING BOOKED! These are formatted as Microsoft Word and Apple Pages files, so you can use them as TEMPLATES to craft your own irresistible TV Press Releases and Segment Pitch documents to get you booked!

And of course you get my personal Rolodex of TV News Producers, Talk Show Producers, and other shows across the USA – *a total of 386 contacts who can book you onto Network television shows, as of this writing!*

There may be other bonuses available too, but the only way to find out is to go to www.NewTVPower.com

ABOUT THE AUTHOR

Clint Arthur is a graduate of the Wharton Business School, a successful entrepreneur with over a decade of experience running his own business, and the bestselling author of "The Last Year Of Your Life," "The Income Doubler," and "What They Teach You At The Wharton Business School." His famous personal transformation experiences and training programs nspire millions of people to go bigger in their life, to amplify their voice, live more intensely, and make a huge impact on the world. He is a much sought-after keynote speaker, and his exploits have been widely reported on in The Wall Street Journal, Los Angeles Times, Time Magazine, and in his frequent Network TV and Radio appearances.

Made in the USA
Charleston, SC
14 December 2011